Education and the middle class

Education and the middle class

SALLY POWER, TONY EDWARDS, GEOFF WHITTY AND VALERIE WIGFALL

Open University Press
Buckingham · Philadelphia

Open University Press
Celtic Court
22 Ballmoor
Buckingham
MK18 1XW

email: enquiries@openup.co.uk
world wide web: www.openup.co.uk

and

325 Chestnut Street
Philadelphia, PA 19106, USA

First Published 2003

A catalogue record of this book is available from the British Library

ISBN 0 335 20555 0 (pb)   0 335 20556 9 (hb)

Library of Congress Cataloging-in-Publication Data
Education and the middle class / Sally Power . . . [et al.].
    p. cm.
    Includes bibliographical references (p.) and index.
    ISBN 0-335-20555-0 (pb) – ISBN 0-335-20556-9 (hb)
      1. Middle class – Education – Great Britain – Longitudinal studies.
    2. Educational surveys – Great Britain. I. Power, Sally.

LC4975.G7 E38   2002
370'.86'220941—dc21   2002072512

Typeset in 10/12pt Sabon by Graphicraft Limited, Hong Kong
Printed in Great Britain by Biddles Limited, Guildford and Kings Lynn

Contents

 Acknowledgements

The research we report in this book began in the 1980s as part of an evaluation of the Assisted Places Scheme funded by the Economic and Social Research Council (grant number C00230036). The four authors later followed up the educational careers and entry into employment of just over half of the 611 children who had been interviewed at the start of their secondary education. The follow-up study was again funded by the ESRC (grant number R000235570). Our greatest debt is to those individuals who took part in the research. Our research made considerable demands on the time and patience of the 347 who responded to a questionnaire that, despite our best efforts, ended up being 21 pages long. Just under half of them also gave willingly of their time for extended interviews in either their homes or places of work. They are of course anonymous in the book, but we hope they hear their voices clearly. All those who participated in the research were sent a copy of our final report to the ESRC. We are grateful to the parents of the young people, who were involved in the earlier research and who helped us to contact their sons and daughters. Our thanks extend also to the schools from the original project who provided us with recent information and whose headteachers were interviewed.

Over the course of the research and afterwards, we have discussed its main themes with many colleagues. We were especially grateful to Basil Bernstein for commenting at length on those parts of the analysis that owe a great deal to his ideas. Other colleagues who have helped us to formulate our ideas include Stephen Ball, Gill Crozier, Miriam David, John Fitz (who was also involved in the earlier research), Sharon Gewirtz, David Halpin, Hugh Lauder, Diane Reay, Carol Vincent and Anne West. We also acknowledge the patience of Open University Press in seeing this project through to publication.

Finally, our thanks go to those who have been of vital assistance in helping us to complete the project and this book, especially Marcia Beer, Carolina Cordero, Cate Knowles, Sophie Kemp and Gaby Critchlow.

1 Destined for success? Political arithmetic and personal narratives

The title of our book is a deliberate echo of *Education and the Working Class*, first published in 1962. That was a biographical study of '88 working class children in a northern industrial city' who went to grammar school and thereby were offered 'the "middle-class" invitations of college, university and the professional career' (Jackson and Marsden 1966: 97). Our own purposes resemble Jackson and Marsden's in that we too are concerned to 'go behind the numbers and feel a way into the various human situations they represent' (1966: 26). Unlike them, however, we have explored the dynamics and dilemmas of 'expected' success, and the 'human situations' of over 300 academically promising individuals who come from predominantly middle-class families. In the early 1980s, shortly after starting secondary school, these individuals and their parents were interviewed about their educational choices and aspirations. Over ten years later, we decided to trace them to explore their progress. In 1995, when they were in their mid-twenties, we sent each of them a long and detailed questionnaire and over the next three years conducted lengthy interviews with nearly half of the respondents (further details of the sample and response rates can be found in Chapter 3).

Their ability, background and schooling made these young people more likely to succeed than to fail. It might be argued that it is an indulgence, even a distraction, to focus on the educationally advantaged when educational inequalities so stubbornly persist. But there are strong grounds for examining relationships between education and the middle class. First, rather little is known about the various ways in which advantage is translated into educational and occupational success. As Butler and Savage (1995: vii) remarked, 'traditionally, the social scientific gaze has been directed either downwards, to the working classes, the poor and the dispossessed, or up-wards, to the wealthy and powerful', and away from 'the more messy and fragmented middle-classes'. This has created an empirical gap more notice-able as the numbers of people deemed to be 'middle class' increase, and as the links between education credentials and high-status employment have tightened.

While we are a long way from Blair's (1999) vision of a one-class Britain, the middle class has certainly grown rapidly. In the early 1960s, 78 per cent of the working population in Jackson and Marsden's 'industrial city' (Huddersfield) were in manual jobs, a proportion only slightly higher than nationally. By the early 1990s, when most of our informants were starting work, a majority of the British workforce was in 'middle-class' employment and about a third in professional or managerial jobs (Mills 1995). This expansion has important implications for the ways in which both educational success and social distinction are defined, reproduced or interrupted.

In sociological theory, the middle class has been internally differentiated by prestige ('upper' and 'lower'); by distinguishing a 'Service Class' of pro-fessional, administrative and managerial employees from an 'Intermediate Class' of routine non-manual workers and a petite bourgeoisie of small-scale proprietors; by market situation as determined by employability, job security and prospects of career progression; by work situation, particularly in relation to levels of autonomy or supervision; and by the kinds of asset or 'capital' which can be transmitted to the next generation. It is the last of these forms of differentiation which largely shaped our own study. And, given the composition of our cohort, we pay particular attention to those middle-class occupations most closely tied to education credentials, and to those sections of the middle class most likely to seek 'the right kind of education' for their children so as to secure a competitive edge in what they regard as 'the main site of social selection' (Lockwood 1995: 3; Power 2000).

But just as the hard line distinguishing 'white collar' and 'blue collar' workers is blurring or at least becoming less relevant, greater access to 'advanced' qualifications has shifted the conventional indicators of educa-tional success and educational failure upwards and made them more opaque. When Jackson and Marsden described how clever working-class children could be transformed into 'middle-class citizens', life chances were power-fully affected by inclusion in or exclusion from the 20 per cent or so deemed capable of 'a grammar school education'. Moreover, only about 4 per cent of the school population went on to higher education. By the time the young men and women in our book were at school, the critical branching points had moved to and beyond the school-leaving age. A majority of 16-year-olds were already remaining in full-time education, while the participation rate in higher education was soon to rise to a third of the age-group.

We also argue that the study of middle-class educational biographies is important analytically. The middle class has tended to appear in educational research as a background against which working-class experiences are contrasted. This leads to untested assertions, especially when it is assumed that 'in discussing the middle class . . . we are considering simply an opposing side of the coin' (Roberts *et al.* 1977: 104). Thus statistical evidence of the extent of working-class failure may overstate the inevitability of middle-class success. The relative invisibility of the middle class reflects the extent to which it has been 'normalized' within the field. In much the same way as 'whiteness' has only recently been granted the same attention as 'blackness', and gender studies have come to focus on masculinity as well as 'women's issues', we argue that issues of class cannot be properly illuminated without giving middle-class educational experience the attention it has largely lacked. Evidence of individual 'human situations' complements, and is likely to complicate, survey data. The retrospective accounts of our informants have enabled us to explore the many ways in which early educational promise was realized, and how opportunities were perceived and taken or declined.

That our respondents' secondary education had been in the traditionally divided system described in the next chapter lent itself in some ways to a political arithmetic approach in the tradition of the Oxford Mobility Studies (Halsey *et al.* 1980). We were certainly interested in how the numbers stacked up to reveal potential structural continuities and discontinuities between the different groups and between them and their parents' generation. Our survey data yielded findings that seemed to demonstrate a clear and apparently consistent influence of types of schooling on subsequent experiences, outcomes and orientations. Yet when we used our interview data to look beyond the aggregate statistics, the results were considerably more complicated. Thus, although political arithmetic helped to provide a useful picture of the general landscape, it did not capture the problematic nature of many transitions, or the instances of unexpected success or failure we encountered, and it risked making unusual transitions appear deviant. This is why we have tried to 'go behind the numbers'. We have therefore sought to reconstruct biographies, but not just for their immediate human interest, absorbing as that often proved to be. This exercise has helped to highlight that, even for middle-class and academically able pupils, transitions which appear 'smooth' in aggregate figures can be anything but smooth for the individuals whose progress the statistics summarize. Indeed, it was one of our more counter-intuitive findings that as many as half of transitions were 'interrupted' in some way, even though the overall picture suggested a fairly unproblematic reproduction of middle-class careers and middle-class identities.

While the individual experiences cited in later chapters raise questions about the 'bigger picture', there is a parallel danger of over-individualizing biographies to the extent that each one is exceptional, with little way of grasping the extent or dimensions of exceptionality. Whitty (1997, 2002) has used the metaphor of the 'vulture's eye' to characterize a distinctively sociological way of looking at educational issues. Apparently a vulture is always able to keep the background landscape in view while enlarging its object of immediate interest. A similar idea was at the heart of C. Wright Mills's (1961) concept of the 'sociological imagination', which involved making connections between biography and history, between identity and structure, and between personal troubles and public issues. Although such formulations do not resolve fundamental questions about the relationship between structure and agency and the extent to which these are distinct aspects of social reality (Giddens 1984; Willmott 1999), they indicate a need for empirical sociology to have multiple foci. Thus Ball (1994: 14) calls for a 'toolbox of diverse concepts and theories' to be used, rather like the different lenses in the vulture's eye, to explore the various elements of social reality at the same time. This is what we have sought to do in our research. Although in reporting our findings we have generally focused in from the aggregate statistics to the individual cases, we have been drawn at times to refine or even redraw the 'bigger picture'. By digging beneath the surface of its landscape, we have sought to understand how its sedimented histories 'get in' to those individual biographies as well as how those individual biographies contribute to a more complex overall picture. In attempting to go beyond both the structural dimensions of the political arithmetic approach and the sheer individuality of biographies as they are 'lived out', we have therefore analysed the data using the diversity of 'concepts and theories' which Ball has argued for.

Helpful in making sense of individual educational biographies were some of the approaches employed in contemporary research into how young people make the 'transitions' to, are 'propelled' into or 'navigate' their way towards their adult occupations and identities (Roberts 1993; Evans and Furlong 1996; Bynner et al. 1997; Hodkinson and Sparkes 1997; Rees et al. 1997; Ball et al. 1999). These have shaped some of the analysis presented in Chapters 7–9. As a metaphor, 'navigation' proved perhaps the most appropriate given the number of interruptions and false starts that half of even our broadly successful cohort experienced. But a new language of description is badly needed to distinguish between different types of 'successful' and 'unsuccessful' educational progressions.

Recent work in class analysis based on rational action theory (Breen and Goldthorpe 1997) addresses why some people choose one pathway and others avoid it. We found it particularly helpful in explaining the careers of our most successful young women because this is where the effects of the restructuring of occupational opportunity were most evident. However, such theories tend to underplay the cultural context in which decisions are made. Although it may appear that the majority of our students had acted 'rationally' in choosing their careers, school and family expectations were often at least as important as, and sometimes overrode, explicit or even implicit calculation of the odds of future material or status gains. We have therefore drawn on various forms of analysis of cultural transactions between home and school to throw light on both continuity and discontinuity in educational progressions. In addition to Bourdieu, the writings of Basil Bernstein in particular seem to provide a way forward in clarifying the various experiences and destinations of our sample of young people as they navigate their way into a fragmented middle class.

Schooling the middle class

Many accounts have been written of the close relationship between the English class structure and the development of the English education system. More often than not, they focus on the emergence of free state schooling and the extent to which inequalities of opportunity persisted despite it. In this chapter, we provide a context for our own research by drawing selectively on these accounts to focus on relationships between the middle class and the changing landscape of education provision. We outline how the middle class has expanded, become internally differentiated and preserved its educational advantages. Given the prominence of private schooling in our cohort, we are especially interested in its characterization in England as not only a middle-class preserve, but a main mechanism for preserving or acquiring social status and 'the entry gate to the class elite that ran British society' (Glennerster 1995: 139).

Hierarchies of schooling

'To arrange types of schooling, whether public or private, in a widely acknowledged hierarchy of academic prestige is also to arrange them in the same order of probability of access for boys of different class origins' (Halsey *et al.* 1980: 70). That relationship was demonstrated through statistical analysis of the educational careers of four male birth cohorts from 1913 to

1952. If we go back to Victorian times, it was taken for granted and made explicit. As our system retains strong residues of Victorian class distinctions, that period makes a convenient starting point for our analysis.

At the highest social level were the nine 'great schools' of Eton, Harrow, Winchester, Rugby, Westminster, Charterhouse, Shrewsbury, Merchant Taylors and St Paul's – the original so-called 'public schools'.[1] These were given in 1864 their own (Clarendon) Commission of Inquiry, which described them as 'the nurseries of our statesmen'. They recruited the sons of almost all prominent landowners, for many of whom it was an almost obligatory rite of passage. In addition, they attracted increasing numbers from the non-landed very rich, for whom it offered status by association, and (particularly Winchester and Rugby) from the higher administrative and professional class (Perkin 1989; Green 1990: 284). At the other end of the social continuum was elementary education, deemed sufficient for the great mass of the 'lower orders' given the political danger of taking them beyond a level at which they could 'appreciate and defer to a higher cultivation when they meet it' (Robert Lowe, quoted in McCulloch 1998: 13). Between those poles, educational provision was uncertain and inadequate for the needs of people of 'middling' wealth and occupations – industrialists, managers and professionals – whose numbers were growing sufficiently for them to appear increasingly as a class (or classes) in their own right. Indeed, they appeared to some commentators to embody the 'substance and sinews' of the country, being 'placed above the atmosphere of mingled suffering and recklessness which poverty creates, and below that of luxurious idleness and self-worship which surrounds great wealth' (Tod 1874: 3).

By contrast, the schooling of their children was in a state of relative neglect. As the influential schools inspector J. G. Fitch (1865: 3) argued, the rich benefited from endowed schools and the poor from parliamentary grants but the middle class was 'cut off from both these resources'. The Newcastle Commission (1861) had investigated 'popular' (that is, working-class) education and the Clarendon Commission elite schooling, but there had been nothing for 'that great mass which lies between them' (Fitch 1865: 3). This was not entirely true in so far as secondary education was then, both in common usage and by official definition, middle-class schooling. But its availability and quality were highly erratic. The investigation Fitch had wanted was carried out by the Schools Inquiry (Taunton) Commission (SIC), which reported in 1868 on a very wide range of endowed, proprietary and private schools. Almost all of them were for boys, and while deploring their generally low standards the Commission urged reforms to reduce the gulf between over 800 endowed schools for boys and 20 for girls (Walford 1993). It ranked the schools, by their curriculum and the socially appropriate origins and destinations of their pupils, in three grades that matched 'roughly, but by no means exactly to the gradations of society'. More accurately they were gradations within the middle class.

The identification of 'first-grade' schools indicates clearly the Commission's sense of differences between the professional and business middle class. These were described (SIC 1868: 16–18) as attracting fathers with 'considerable income independent of their own exertions', or whose profits from business or one of the more lucrative professions 'put them on the same level'. But they also drew some of the 'poorer gentry' and the more poorly paid professions (the Church, the law and medicine), who, having 'received a cultivated education themselves, have nothing to look to but education to keep their sons on a high social level'. They included the more reputable endowed grammar schools, some of which had followed the example set by Harrow, Rugby and Shrewsbury by becoming boarding schools with national intakes which crowded out the 'poor and needy scholars' envisaged by their founders (Tapper 1997: 28–53). They also included newly created 'public schools' – Cheltenham, Radley, Marlborough, Clifton and Wellington were examples – which never pretended to be other than socially selective, but which also promised (as the first headmaster of Radley put it) to 'confer an aristocracy on boys who do not inherit it' (quoted in Honey 1977: 228).

Lower in esteem were a variety of other proprietary and endowed schools, their clientele overlapping with that of the 'first grade' but also patronized by 'the larger shopkeepers, rising men of business and the larger tenant farmers'. These usually had a more modern, less classics-dominated, curriculum and a normal leaving age of 16 rather than 18, and were rarely followed by university.

Schools placed in the third grade provided for a middle class 'distinctly lower in scale' and even for some better-off working-class families, who wished their sons to acquire 'very good skills in reading, writing and arithmetic' (SIC 1868: 18). Their clienteles included 'smaller tenant farmers, the small tradesmen, the superior artisans', and were likely to return their pupils to the same occupational levels. That this lowest grade included some ancient grammar schools incapable of providing much more than an elementary education was deplored by the Commission, which urged the prompt removal of restrictions on admissions and curriculum maintained by sticking pedantically to foundation charters. Those which subsequently managed to promote themselves from this third grade tended to be 'annexed' by securely middle-class parents (Tapper 1997: 40).

Despite some extensions into the upper class at one end of the continuum and into the 'respectable' working class at the other, secondary education was effectively middle-class schooling. As an analysis of intakes from the later Victorian period indicated, most even of the public schools were 'purely and simply schools for the middle classes and, often, for the lower middle class' (Rubinstein 1986: 173). There may have been by then 'a large new section of the middle class . . . composed of shareholders, not individual owners', which was rich enough to afford the fees at leading schools and 'no longer class conscious enough' to avoid them (Mack 1941: 121). But the 'pool' of potential middle-class clients so far exceeded the roughly 20,000 places available in 'recognized' public schools by the end of the century that most middle-class families had chosen none of them, the northern middle class and businessmen generally being substantially under-represented in their intakes (Berghoff 1990; Rubinstein 1993). Although new schools were emerging and old endowed schools being reformed, supply continued to be outpaced by demand. This mattered increasingly as 'middle-class' employment both expanded and became rather more dependent on some accredited academic achievement.

Beginning in the 1850s with competitive entry to the Indian Civil Service, there was a slow shift from private patronage to public examinations in determining access to national and imperial administration, and to the 'higher' professions. Academic achievement was not essential as long as notions of 'careers open to talent' continued to be circumscribed by reliance, especially in relation to 'officer class' positions in the imperial services and the City, on the 'right kind of man' from the right kind of family and school. But the rapid growth in state functions itself created new opportunities for upward social mobility. Between 1881 and 1901, for example, the number of males employed in 'general and local government' increased from 97,000 to 172,000, and the number of females from 7000 to 26,000. Also significant for women as at least 'respectable' employment was the increase over those 20 years from 6000 to 56,000 in the numbers employed as 'commercial and business clerks', and between the 1870 Education Act and the late 1890s from 12,000 to 53,000 certificated teachers (Lawson and Silver 1973). The Oxford and Cambridge 'Local' Examinations, introduced in 1858–59 and initially called 'middle class examinations', provided secondary schools with standards against which to demonstrate their capacity to prepare pupils for desirable employment and so appeal to parents who most 'looked to' education to secure respectability or better for their children (Roach 1971). Those fearful that greater reliance on examinations would exclude from desirable occupations many traditional recruits from 'the best families' were reassured by Gladstone that 'natural gifts' and 'acquired advantages' would only be reinforced by good schooling, thereby constituting a continuing and 'immense' superiority (quoted in Roach 1971: 193).

While there was broad agreement about the need for more distinctive middle-class schooling, there were deep differences over whether the gap between supply and demand could be filled through increasing private provision, or whether it required state intervention. Robert Lowe, the architect of reformed elementary instruction, argued in 1868 that the middle class 'would not think of sending its children to primary schools supported by the state, and is not yet in the condition of life to think of sending its children to universities'; expanding secondary education should be left to private enterprise, and state support confined to the poor. In contrast, and a generation later, Matthew Arnold asked:

> Why cannot we have throughout England – as the French have throughout France, as the Germans have throughout Germany, as the Swiss have throughout Switzerland, as the Dutch have throughout Holland – schools where the children of our middle and professional classes may obtain an education of as good a quality . . . as the education which the French children of the corresponding class obtain?
>
> (Arnold 1892: 37–8)

To rely on the 'principle of supply and demand to do for us all we want in providing education', Arnold argued, 'is to lean upon a broken reed' (1892: 43).

As so often in British education, reforms were a compromise between laissez-faire and state involvement in revising school endowments, inspecting quality and promoting or at least permitting 'higher elementary' provision in the cities. But meritocratic justifications for expanding the 'middle' of the system were slow to develop, obscured by fears that the middle class would be overtaken by the increasingly educated working class. As a pamphleteer had warned in 1861:

> The class below you are advancing with a slow indeed, but a steady step; you can already, some of you, hear the tread. How will it be when their intelligence, knowledge and power of mind shall equal and surpass yours? What is to be looked for if you place a pyramid on its apex?
>
> (Anon 1861: 53)

There were those like Fitch (1865) who argued that ability deserved assistance wherever it was found. The Girls' Public Day Schools Trust, for example, was founded in 1871 to educate 'girls of all classes above the elementary', with the declared purpose of enabling the ablest of them to compete with males both academically and for entry to a very slowly widening range of professional employment (Kamm 1971). At an official level, even the class-conscious Taunton Commission had cautiously suggested 'some mode of selection by merit' through which selected working-class boys might show that they would 'use with advantage the education usually given to gentlemen'. Towards the end of the century, and although still assuming secondary education to be both middle class and internally stratified, the Bryce Commission (1895) was more enthusiastic in proposing 'ample provision for enabling selected children of the poorer parents to climb the educational ladder'. It was this notion of a ladder which weakened the middle-class monopoly of secondary education.

Academic and social selection

Following the legislation of 1902, LEA-maintained grammar schools for girls as well as boys were established in almost every major centre of population and presented as the embodiment of progressive reform. They provided an academic preparation for at least white-collar work, and for a very small minority the prospect of university and a professional career. Provision was further increased by those established secondary schools which accepted some state funding on the accompanying condition that they made no fewer than 25 per cent of their places free to suitably able children. What Sydney Webb called the 'capacity catching' function of 'scholarship' examinations was intended both to draw more deeply on the 'pool of ability' in the national interest and to base individual opportunity on academic merit. In pursuit of those objectives the new science of mental measurement rapidly gained momentum, defended by one of its pioneers, Godfrey Thomson, as the best way 'of helping children of intelligence who might otherwise be overlooked'. Thus his own Northumberland Mental Test replaced the previous free place examinations, which he argued had favoured children from 'comparatively well-to-do and more cultured homes' in residential districts near Newcastle, discouraging parents and teachers in less advantaged areas 'from entering children at all' (Thomson 1969: 100–1).

The Victorian reforms had 'circumscribed the meritocratic principle to exclude the majority of the population' because, far from 'creating a normative form of middle class education as the French lycée and American high school had at least partially done', they had 'perpetuated and intensified' differences within the middle class (Green 1990: 291). Changes after 1902 continued this 'social and cultural fragmentation', most obviously by dividing middle-class families who remained outside state provision from those for whom it provided an acceptable alternative to private schooling. This was not only because fees were generally considerably lower than in the public schools. There were also free places, the proportion of which had risen in England to 46 per cent by 1938, with wide variations between local authorities. As they were not means-tested until the introduction of some 'special places' in the 1930s, middle-class families took advantage of them, especially as they were often turned down by working-class families unable to support the indirect costs and the obligation to consider schooling well beyond the minimum leaving age of 14 which was attached to a free place. If secondary education was no longer a middle-class 'preserve', it remained a predominantly middle-class experience.

Mack (1941: 255) therefore made the social contrasts too sharp when he defined public schools as 'non-local endowed boarding schools for the upper classes', and described the 'new secondary schools' as catering 'on the whole to a different social class'. Many public schools experienced a sufficient diversion of middle-class demand to create real anxiety about their future viability. The Fleming Committee, appointed in 1942 to explore how they could be made 'accessible to all classes irrespective of wealth and social position', was initiated from within that sector in the hope of new publicly funded custom (Gosden 1976: 332–8). Even though most were again full when the time came to implement the Committee's proposals for state-aided boarding education, so that any benefits were seen as outweighed by the consequent costs to independence and social exclusiveness, the claim that private schooling has consistently been 'the main means of transferring economic status, social position and influence from generation to generation' (Labour Party 1980: 10) is not supported by evidence. It ignores the high proportions of even upper middle-class families who did not choose it for their sons, and the even larger proportion of 'incomers' who have not had the benefits it is assumed to bestow. Oxford Mobility Study data for the decades before and after the introduction of free 'secondary education for all' in 1944 showed that a majority of professionals, managers and proprietors had used the state sector at the more critical secondary stage, and that it was those at the higher levels whose choices of public or private had 'scattered' most widely (Halsey *et al.* 1980: 71). The statistics in Table 2.1 show very unequal access to selective secondary education, although it is important to note that, while middle-class children were certainly at a large relative advantage, more than half of those born before 1920 in families of the professionally employed did not experience the benefits it promised.

These figures also illustrate the increased provision after 1944 for children identified as of 'grammar school ability'. Although this was intended to limit social class differences to what could be justified on academic merit, social selection persisted. Longitudinal research into the consequent

Table 2.1 Class inequalities of opportunity for entry to selective secondary education, England and Wales

Social origin (father's occupation)	Percentage of children who obtained education in grammar and independent schools among those born				
	Before 1910	1910–19	1920–29	Late 1930s	Approx. 1957–60
Professional and managerial	37	47	52	62	47
Other non-manual and skilled manual	7	13	16	20	22
Semi-skilled and unskilled	1	4	7	10	10
All children	12	16	18	23	25

Source: Westergaard and Resler (1975).

redistribution of opportunities suggested that the immediate effect had been to 'increase subsidies to the affluent', and to intensify pressure from middle-class families for access to the only esteemed part of the tripartitite system (Halsey *et al.* 1980: 210).

Large numbers of working-class children did of course gain entry to grammar schools, the great majority of whose pupils were 'first-generation' in schools of that kind (Halsey *et al.* 1980). The claim that they continued to be 'middle-class schools' was dismissed as 'ridiculous' on the grounds that two-thirds of their entrants by the late 1950s came from working-class families, and that the skilled working class was statistically 'almost perfectly represented' (Musgrove 1979: 107). In fact there were large variations over time, between local authorities and between neighbouring schools. Children from middle-class families tended to be highly over-represented where and when competition for grammar school places was most severe (Blackburn and Marsh 1991). Some 'neighbourhood' grammar schools drew from their location mainly working-class intakes, whereas others recruited mainly middle-class pupils either from a socially segregated area or because their reputation attracted applicants from a wide 'catchment'. This diversity is illustrated most clearly by the direct-grant grammar schools. These were both praised for their heterogeneity because they were less socially exclus-ive than most entirely fee-paying schools (Cobban 1969) and criticized because they were more exclusive than state grammar schools (Public Schools Commission 1970: 117). Both praise and blame were over-generalized. Whereas the academic excellence attributed to the leading schools was inseparable from intakes which were both 'predominantly middle class' and drawn largely from within the top 5 per cent of the ability range (Saran 1973; Halsey *et al.* 1980: 57), there were some (mainly Catholic) direct-grant schools which were less selective both academically and socially than maintained grammar schools nearby.

Making all places free in state-maintained grammar schools after 1944 had brought complaints that the entry of less 'cultivated' children carried the risk of falling academic and cultural standards. Some people argued that fee-paying had enabled middle-class parents to feel a sense of pride that they were bestowing advantages on their children (Davis 1967). In lamenting the decline of the middle class, Lewis and Maude (1949: 237–8) noted that 'the middle-class taxpayer' would now have the dubious satis-faction of knowing 'that his struggles to earn enough money to educate his children as he wished were also educating everybody else's children to an equivalent degree of privilege'. The quality of English public and private secondary education, they argued, had come from 'concentrating boys and girls, mainly from the middle classes, in one set of schools', and there were limits to how many 'of what we may, for the sake of a short phrase, call "rank outsiders"' could safely be absorbed without penalizing 'those whose parents are already struggling up the social ladder'.

The wish to preserve social selectivity led sections of the middle class to continue to pay for secondary education even though boarding and day fees in public schools rose significantly above the rate of inflation in most post-war years. Although by the 1960s enough private schools had failed or were surviving precariously to raise hopes that rising standards of state education would eventually make the sector irrelevant, such optimism ignored the strength of demand for its leading schools and the relative security of many more. There was certainly no weakening of what the Public Schools Commission (1968) noted regretfully as their 'close association with particular classes'. The social exclusiveness maintained by high fees was not lowered significantly by school scholarships, state bursaries for children of 'officer class' parents posted abroad on government service and local authority buying of places for children 'in need of' boarding education. Contemporary research indicated that such limited sponsorship did 'almost nothing' to widen the schools' social range because, although as many as one pupil in five received some financial help with the costs of private schooling, only one in eight paid less than 95 per cent of 'full' fees (Glennerster and Wilson 1970: 47). Even a study commissioned by the Headmasters' Conference to dispel 'mists of prejudice and ignorance' about educational privilege revealed a large minority of pupils who were first generation fee-payers but also estimated that only some 3 per cent of the total, and only 10 per cent even in day schools, were not from middle-class families (Kalton 1966).

That support for private schooling survived the growth and academic success of state grammar schools suggests a clientele whose custom did not have to be earned because for them state schooling remained unthinkable, and a clientele which continued to assume distinctive benefits which made fee-paying seem a good investment. Confidence that private schooling conferred relative advantages did not entail unanimity about what those advantages were. It had rather different appeal for different sections of the middle class and, as we show in detail in Chapter 3, its predominant appeal has changed substantially over time. At this point we want to explore, briefly, Bernstein's (1977: 18) suggestion that the English middle class had not only been able to preserve its generally privileged educational position, but was unique in having developed through private schooling 'differentiated forms of socialization' that had effects on its internal structure and culture 'worthy of prolonged study'.

At the institutional level, for example, Rubinstein's (1993) analysis of alumni registers from leading public schools indicated that Eton had been the 'school par excellence of aristocrats and the wealthy' and Harrow more open to 'new money', that Winchester and Rugby had appealed to 'poor but still well-established sections of the gentry and (especially) the professional classes' who hoped for occupational success through academic achievement and that Mill Hill's non-conformist origins had attracted the widest range of wealth and income. To them can be added the appeal of new 'progressive' private schools like Dartington Hall and Sidcot, 'peopled by what the conservative leaders of the public schools could consider merely as the lunatic fringe of the upper classes' (Mack 1941: 379) and later described as attracting 'disaffected intellectuals' (Salter and Tapper 1985: 51). Broad distinctions can be drawn between the more diffuse 'character-building' purposes of many boarding schools, schools where new wealth was 'converted into cultural assets for the next generation' (Scott 1991: 115) without great emphasis on qualifications, and the academic orientation of leading private day schools. And they can be drawn between the 'finishing school' tradition in girls' private schooling and the overt 'education feminism' which challenged gender constraints on what girls should study and aspire to and which was characteristic of the Girls' Public Day Schools Trust. More generally still, and clearly related to the transmission of different forms of family capital, it was unsurprising that the Oxford Mobility Study showed that boys from salaried professional families had been relatively more prominent in the more academic direct-grant schools, and boys from self-employed and business class families in private schools that gave less obvious priority to academic success (Halsey *et al.* 1980).

It was an emphasis on academic results, however, that came to shape at least those upper reaches of the private sector which have preoccupied researchers. The origins of an 'academic revolution' are usually traced back to the increasing success of state grammar schools in preparing pupils for entry to prestigious universities and occupations (Rae 1981). It was intensified by the pace of comprehensive reorganization. Comparative research has shown a clear link between the availability of academic and social selectiveness within the state system, and the proportion of middle-class families willing to pay for schooling (Walford 1989). And while middle-class parents were disproportionately successful in getting their children into grammar schools, the provision of places at roughly 20 per cent of the age group fell far short of demand even before comprehensive reorganization. It is intensified competition for grammar school places, and parental fears of being allocated a place in a secondary modern school, that partly explains the rapid acceptance of comprehensive education. Yet it is the rapid disappearance of grammar schools from the state sector that is also seen as producing a middle-class 'decampment' into private schooling (Adonis and Pollard 1998). In the rest of this chapter, we examine these claims of cause and effect.

The middle class and comprehensive schooling

The introduction and spread of comprehensive schools is often accounted for as bringing a widening of opportunity for working-class pupils. Indeed, some opponents interpreted the entire process as the victory of deluded egalitarianism over solid middle-class values (Davis 1967; Hutber 1976). Another explanation can be found in the anxieties of middle-class parents themselves. It is in the battle over comprehensive education that we also see a distinct split between sections of the middle class.

In a case study of comprehensive schooling that became something of a citation classic, Ford (1969: 5–6) argued that fairly substantial numbers of middle-class families were experiencing for the first time the effects of their children 'receiving an "inferior" education, and one which was not generally intended as preparation for middle class occupations'.

> Since the majority of secondary modern children have always been from working class homes and their low educational status, and consequent low anticipations of occupational status, have been quite in accord with their parents' occupational prestige, we would not expect them or their parents to define their circumstances as unjust. The *consistently* deprived group then is not a likely source of pressure for change; our search for an explanation of the innovation in educational attitudes becomes the search for a *marginal* group: a group with inconsistent status rankings.
>
> (Emphasis in original)

To the extent that state grammar schools provided the main means of social ascent through education 'throughout the middle ranges of the class system' (Turner 1961), then failure to secure a place sharply depressed the 'realistic' career expectations of both children and their parents. A contemporary study of the career aspirations and expectations of children before and after taking the decisive 11-plus tests concluded that the outcomes had more effect than family background, the children displaying 'a startlingly accurate appraisal of life chances . . . and a shrewd appreciation of the social and economic implications of their placing' within an openly stratified system (Liversidge 1962: 27). Their 'shrewdness' was confirmed by the Oxford Mobility Study's demonstration that working-class boys who gained entry to grammar schools had much better chances of Service Class jobs than did middle-class boys who 'failed' the 11-plus (Halsey *et al.* 1980: 127–36). Middle-class families may have gained a disproportionate share of grammar school places, but those working-class boys who 'climbed the scholarship ladder . . . had embarked on the first stage of an extraordinary ascent' (Heath and Ridge 1983: 242). For middle-class families, in particular those with only cultural capital to pass on, it was a matter of avoiding any unfortunate descent.

Fears of 'descent' brought middle-class support for ending the 11-plus. As an illustration of the coexistence of relative advantage with considerable risks, a comparison of pass rates from two local authorities reported that, while only 2 per cent of children from social class VI passed the test, 46 per cent of those from social class I and a majority (62 per cent) from social class II failed it (Swift 1965). Support for comprehensive education was class-related in that more middle-class parents were 'against' it than working-class parents, but a Research Services opinion poll published in *New Society* in 1967 showed a majority 'in favour' (46 per cent to 37 per cent) among the middle-class respondents (Ford 1969: 7). It is true that middle-class parents in some areas took the lead in organizing local resistance to the disappearance of grammar schools, or in insisting on the preservation of 'successful' selective schools within an ostensibly comprehensive local system (Kerckhoff *et al.* 1997). But suburbanization also had sufficiently 'discrete social layers' in many areas (Perkin 1989: 269) that some 'neighbourhood' comprehensive schools could be 'colonized' by predominantly middle-class intakes, and so provide a safer prospect than the risks attending 11-plus selection (Walford and Jones 1986). Even where intakes were more socially mixed, middle-class children could continue to receive a relatively 'privileged' educational experience through various streaming and banding arrangements, by which they were disproportionately concentrated in the higher-ability groupings to an extent that could be more sharply class aligned than entry to grammar schools had been (Ball 1981).

There have been claims, most recently by Adonis and Pollard (1998), that fear of falling standards in a state system which no longer offered an extensive grammar school escape has led to a 'mass decampment' of middle-class families into private schooling. In their analysis, Adonis and Pollard 'matched' the 610,000 pupils in the private sector in the mid-1990s with the 740,000 school-aged children recorded in the 1991 Census as coming from professional, managerial and skilled non-manual households. They noted that two-thirds of *all* private school pupils came from the higher socio-economic level, that lists of the 'thousand best' secondary schools published annually (in the *Financial Times*, for example) consist overwhelmingly of those in the private sector; and concluded that 'the character of today's class meritocracy is clear' (Adonis and Pollard 1998: 24, 39).

However, their conclusion is based on a narrow definition of private schooling and of the middle class. They ignore the growing numbers of evangelical Christian, Muslim, black, small and other private schools that are not selective, not expensive and not associated with social advantage in either the typical origins or typical destinations of their pupils (Walford 1991; Gorard 1997). They also refer mainly to those fractions of a growing middle class employed in the City and its connected professions, which they saw as increasingly distanced in income, wealth and education, from the white-collar middle class. It is the children of this 'super-class' that they locate almost entirely in a private sector more socially segregated not only than in other countries but than previously even in England.

This may partly explain why other statistics seem to contradict their thesis. While the ratio of private to public expenditure on education certainly increased significantly between the late 1970s and the early 1990s, the supply of private schooling did not rise to meet demand from the growing and (in parts) more affluent middle class, as a crude market logic might predict. Between 1951 and 1981, private sector numbers remained fairly steady despite two sharp rises in the age-group in the late 1950s and early 1970s. Its market share then rose over the next ten years from 6.6 to 8.1 per cent of 11- to 15-year-olds, and has remained since at roughly that level. Protected by their charitable status from the full force of market pressures, popular private schools appear to have chosen not to expand but to become more selective, which is a rational strategy for schools marketing academic excellence (Halsey *et al.* 1984: 16).

Nevertheless, Adonis and Pollard's work does highlight the need to explore further divisions within the middle class, of which their own 'super-class' is but one, and the implications of these divisions for choice of schooling, which we examine in the chapter that follows.

Note

1 We use the term 'public school' here in the traditional English sense of an élite private school. The term 'private school' is used to describe any school in the private sector, including these public schools.

3 Choosing the 'right' school

Since the 1988 Education Reform Act, the English education system has been extensively restructured on market principles. Political justifications for these changes, and ensuing research into their consequences, often seem to assume that parental choice and diversity of provision are new phenomena. Yet interviews with over 400 parents in the early 1980s indicated that middle-class parents in particular already had a strong sense of themselves as 'education consumers'. Most had spent considerable time and effort weighing up the various options, even where their eventual choice had been based more on stereotyping than on information about the alternatives (Edwards *et al.* 1989: 196–9).

At the time when our informants' parents were choosing a secondary school, there was of course less formal diversity than now. Within the state-maintained sector about one child in ten still went to a grammar school, while voluntary-aided church schools could determine their own admissions policies. But city technology colleges, grant maintained schools and specialist schools had yet to appear, and entry to comprehensive schools was still determined by catchment area in many localities. However, the contexts for making the 'right choice' of school had changed significantly since Jackson and Marsden (1966) associated state grammar schools with the 'middle-class invitations' of higher education and professional or managerial employment. Very few parents had attended comprehensive schools themselves, and sometimes relied heavily on image and rumour. The rapid disappearance of state grammar schools had enabled a private sector, reinforced by the decision of most direct-grant grammar schools, to become 'fully' independent to market 'academic excellence', and produced those 'pragmatic' converts to fee-paying described by Fox (1984), who looked to that sector for the kind of schooling they believed to be no longer available in the state system (Edwards and Whitty 1997). And as we emphasize in the next chapter, the 'middle-class invitations' identified by Jackson and Marsden were much more dependent on advanced qualifications than they had been in the 1960s.

The schools

In this and the three following chapters, we examine the pathways taken by our informants through 18 different secondary schools, nine private and nine state-maintained. These schools were not intended to be representative either of the system at large or even of major divisions within it. The original research had been an evaluation of the Assisted Places Scheme, so that the private schools had to be of sufficient quality to justify claims that the places they were allocated were restoring educational opportunities unavailable in the public sector. Indeed, the fact that many schools initially interested in offering places had been rejected as lacking sufficient academic credibility is a useful corrective to the association of generally high standards with private schooling (Edwards *et al.* 1989: 41–4). Our nine private schools had certainly passed that test, five of them subsequently appearing regularly in lists of the hundred 'best schools' as identified by non-value-added examination results. Not surprisingly, given their long tradition of entry on academic merit, former direct-grant grammar schools provided nearly three-quarters of the places available in the Scheme's first year, and two-thirds of the 55,000 places available when it was fully in operation in 1986. Six of our nine private schools were from that category. The emphasis placed on the Scheme providing an escape route from the mediocrity attributed to comprehensive education in the rhetoric meant that the state schools we chose to include in the earlier study were from the same local networks as those offering assisted places. Although most of our informants came from middle-class homes, the seven comprehensives were typical of that extremely mixed category in their variety of intake, performance and ethos. The two maintained grammar schools were in local authorities which had still retained 11-plus academic selection. Table 3.1 shows the distribution of the original cohort, and of that part of it we followed up some 12 years later, across the three broad types of secondary school.

Differences between and within the types of schools can be represented in a rough hierarchy based on prestige and on academic and social exclusiveness. Table 3.2 sets out that hierarchy, using the same institutional

Table 3.1 Distribution of the original and later cohorts

	Original cohort	Later cohort
Elite private	68	36
Respectable private	232	139
State grammar	51	34
Comprehensive	233	138
Total	584	347

We had 584 usable records from our original sample of 611 and 80 per cent (469/584) of these were traced and sent questionnaires designed to gather data on basic socio-economic indicators, educational achievements, school experiences, subsequent careers and cultural and political dispositions. The length of the questionnaire (21 pages) and high levels of transience of our sample contributed to a slow response rate. Subsequent chasings eventually produced 347 completed returns: 59 per cent of the cohort and 74 per cent of those who were traced. These constituted a representative sample of the original group in terms of sex, sector of school and mode of sponsorship. A profile of non-respondents and untraceable members of the cohort (constructed from our original data and school information) reveals that they share a similar socio-economic profile to those who responded, though those with fathers in middle rank occupations were somewhat underrepresented. Where school records of non-respondents' educational achievements and destinations exist, they suggest a similar pattern to those of our respondents.

Table 3.2 A hierarchy of provision

Elite private
Cathedral College	13–18 boys' public school with boarding (700 pupils)
Bankside College	13–18 boys' public school with boarding (600 pupils)
St Hilda's	11–18 girls' public school (600 pupils)

Respectable private
Nortown Grammar	11–18 ex-direct-grant boys' school (1400 pupils)
Dame Margaret's	11–18 girls' school (550 pupils)
Nortown High	11–18 ex-direct-grant girls' school (500 pupils)
Milltown Grammar	11–18 ex-direct-grant boys' school (650 pupils)
Milltown High	11–18 ex-direct-grant girls' school (500 pupils)
Weston	13–18 boys' school with boarding (300 pupils)

State grammar
| Highgrove County | 11–18 grammar school for girls (1000 pupils) |
| Archbishop Ambrose | 11–18 grammar school for boys (850 pupils) |

Comprehensive
Shirebrook	13–18 coeducational (1000 pupils)
Vicarage Road	11–16 coeducational (950 pupils)
Parkside	11–16 girls' school (950 pupils)
Cherry Tree	11–18 coeducational (1500 pupils)
Rowton	11–18 coeducational (1600 pupils)
Frampton	11–18 coeducational (800 pupils)
Moorside	11–18 coeducational (1500 pupils)

pseudonyms as in the original study. At the top are three undoubtedly 'elite' schools with long-established national reputations. Below them in social status, though not in academic performance, are the former direct-grant schools and a fully independent school with a similar intake, which enjoyed at least very strong local standing. A fourth private school occupies a more ambiguous position; with a majority of boarders and few assisted places its fee levels ensured a socially selective intake, but its orientation was less conspicuously academic and reflected the relatively diffuse purposes still characterizing parts of the private sector. The two grammar schools are placed next as the most obvious state-provided alternative to fee paying. The seven comprehensive schools varied enough to make their categorical location very heterogeneous, but we have not attempted to 'rank' them.

School-level academic performance was not then as visible, and therefore as apparently comparable, as local league tables and lists of 'best schools' have made it since. But there were other significant differences between the schools, which, while certainly related to their selectiveness, reflect different values and assumptions about the nature of schooling. These cultural differences are also important for understanding our parents' decisions about where to send their children, and we use Bernstein's analytical framework to explore them.

School cultures: instrumental and expressive orders

In terms of school cultures, Bernstein (1977) identified two distinct but interrelated complexes of behaviours. The expressive order is the complex of behaviour and activities to do with conduct, character and manner. Before the 'academic revolution' mentioned in the previous chapter and discussed more fully in the next, it was to this that many parents looked for the self-confidence and personal style they attributed to private schooling. The instrumental order is concerned with the acquisition of specific skills and bodies of knowledge. By the 1990s, the Independent Schools' Information Service (ISIS 1994: 32) defined the principal appeal of its member institutions in entirely instrumental terms – as a matter of high standards, good teaching and small classes. Within individual schools, there can be variation in the relative strengths of each of these orders, and there may be considerable tension between them. Bernstein's distinction between them enabled him to differentiate between an informed understanding and acceptance of both means and ends, which was easier for middle-class pupils, and an acceptance of the instrumental benefits of academic success 'detached' from any wider educational commitment. He also drew attention, however, to 'estranged' middle-class pupils who accept the ends but lack the ability or motivation to achieve them, some of whom appear in our later chapters. There is also another dimension to be considered in trying to categorize individual institutions. Both the instrumental and the expressive orders tend towards being 'open' or 'closed', leading to social relations within the school that are predominantly 'differentiated' or 'stratified'.

Before positioning our schools within that analytical framework, we recognize that King's (1976, 1981) research led him to conclude that Bernstein's distinction between 'open' and 'closed' schools was too vague to provide an adequate basis for categorization, but that the survey methods he used may have been inappropriate for testing Bernstein's propositions (Tyler 1988). For what follows, we complemented our informants' retrospective accounts of their schooling with schools' published information, our visits and interviews with headteachers, and with parental and pupil views gathered during the initial study. The emphasis and specific attributes of each school were then compared and ranked relative to each other along two axes to indicate the strength of the instrumental and expressive order respectively within each school's culture. From our analysis of the data, the following range of school types shown in Figure 3.1 emerged.

There is a close connection between the culture of a school and its pupil composition as controlled through its own or its local authority's admissions policies and practices. Those schools highest on the instrumental side, and with strong stratificatory structures, were academically selective state-maintained and former direct-grant. They were also single-sex. Conversely, most of the schools which tended to emphasize the expressive order, especially on principles of differentiation, were state-maintained comprehensive schools and were coeducational. The 'elite' schools tended to occupy a wider range of positions. Bankside College and Weston School placed relatively greater emphasis on the expressive order than the other private schools but, unlike the comprehensives, did so with an emphasis on hierarchy and competition through activities such as team games and combined cadet corps. There was certainly little of that training in flexibility and negotiation which Walford (1986) attributed to the extra-curriculum of elite schools and identified as suitable preparation for future leadership positions.

To illustrate this outline, we compare three schools with different admissions policies and histories – St Hilda's, Archbishop Ambrose and Vicarage Road – to represent contrasting school cultures.

St Hilda's, Archbishop Ambrose and Vicarage Road

St Hilda's was an 'elite' private school with a foundation dating back to the sixteenth century. When some of our informants started there in the early 1980s, there were just under 600 11–18-year-olds on the register. It had its own small preparatory school but recruited from across the city, mainly from within the private sector. Even though high fees and high academic entry standards brought a great deal of self-selection among applicants, there was (and still is) fierce competition for places. Three girls took the

+ Strength of instrumental order

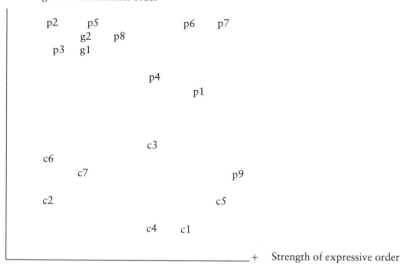

Key: c, comprehensive; g, state grammar; p, private.

p1	Bankside College	g1	Highgrove County
p2	Milltown Grammar	g2	Archbishop Ambrose
p3	Milltown High	c1	Frampton
p4	Dame Margaret's	c2	Cherry Tree
p5	Nortown Grammar	c3	Shirebrook
p6	St Hilda's	c4	Rowton
p7	Cathedral College	c5	Vicarage Road
p8	Nortown High	c6	Moorside
p9	Weston	c7	Parkside

Figure 3.1 The culture of the 18 research schools

entrance examination for every place offered, and they were both inter-viewed and tested in mathematics and English. The then headteacher com-mented that potential recruits were asked to sit in on an art and a science lesson so that 'we see how they are in the class situation being taught, how they relate to each other, how they take in information that they've never had before, how they push it back because we give them each a little test.'

Once girls were accepted, however, the culture of the school was relatively permissive and open. High academic performance was certainly celebrated, but in relation to a broad curriculum and in more than its instrumental aspects. A follow-up visit to the school indicated that it was then considering the introduction of philosophy through all the year groups, and the current prospectus referred to 'keeping doors open' and to the avoidance of 'early specialisation and premature commitment'. There is no streaming within the school and internal examinations, the prospectus claims, are 'deliberately kept to a minimum'. The expressive side is (and was) actively encouraged, with pupils obliged, for example, to attend speech and drama lessons and to join school societies. The school is nationally renowned for its music, and has a purpose-built music wing, two orchestras, a wind band and several choirs. There is little overt emphasis on discipline. The present prospectus refers to voluntary conformity to the norms of the school, rules 'are kept to a minimum' and 'in seeking to maintain a liberal atmosphere in which girls can develop high personal standards and disciplined habits of work, the school relies in large measure on the co-operation of parents and girls which it has always enjoyed.' Particularly noteworthy is the fact that there is no school uniform: 'girls are expected to dress sensibly for school and to avoid extremes.'

Archbishop Ambrose was an ex-direct-grant grammar school for boys which then became LEA-maintained and subsequently grant-maintained. When our respondents were there, it had 850 boys. Most pupils stayed on into the sixth form, entry rates to university were high and considerable numbers went to Oxford or Cambridge. There was a pronounced instrumental emphasis. Thus the school prospectus in the early 1980s provided little more than a list of subjects and options, complemented by further lists of extra-curricular activities and disciplinary procedures. Both instrumental and expressive orders can also be classified as strongly stratified, both internally and externally. In Bernstein's terms, the instrumental order was constructed along lines of closure and competition. An already highly selected intake was further subdivided within the school in terms of subject-based ability. Homework requirements were heavy, and examination performance was emphasized.

On the expressive side, relations between staff and pupils, and between pupils, were clearly demarcated, with various age-differentiated rituals. For example, pupils wore different versions of the uniform as they progressed through the school. In the fifth year (Year 11), a different badge had to be worn on the blazer, the colour and badge of which changed again in the sixth form. The marking-off of the school's students from those of other schools, and from contemporary youth culture, was evident in the strict guidelines on appearance: footwear 'not suede', scarves 'only of regulation colour', hair 'will be of reasonable bulk' and 'sideburns will not extend below the earlobe'. Extra-curricular activities also emphasized hierarchy, regimentation and competition. In addition to inter-house competitions, pupils could participate in the Venture Scout unit and in general knowledge competitions.

Vicarage Road was a coeducational comprehensive school. In the early 1980s it had over 900 students aged 11–16. A former secondary modern school, it had made vigorous efforts to throw off negative associations from its past and to recruit parents, particularly middle-class parents, from both the borough and the adjacent authority. By comparison with Archbishop Ambrose, it was far weaker on the instrumental side and stronger on the expressive side. Both dimensions tended to be structured along lines of openness rather than closure, thereby contributing to differentiated rather than stratified social relations within the school and a more diffuse approach to student well-being.

The instrumental order was less prominent in school literature, and less of a main theme in interviews with the then headteacher. Teaching groups were heterogeneous, with less internal screening and weaker boundaries. Many classes, at least in the initial stages, were taken in tutor groups constructed to offer a range of ability. Of course, as Bernstein pointed out, schools may differentiate their students as they progress so as to offer those identified as 'able' a different curriculum and a different pedagogy (Bernstein 1990: 52). Our informants were among the school's most academically able pupils, and the instrumental order was likely to have been more stratified and less differentiated for them than for 'less able' contemporaries. At least in the early years, traditional subject specialisms were much less visible (in Bernstein's terms, less strongly classified) than at Archbishop Ambrose, being clustered into areas such as humanities, creative studies and communication skills. There was also less closure to outside influences. As the headteacher commented: 'We offer a very much wider curriculum and the social education and the youngsters who actually emerge are far better prepared for the sort of life they are going to lead.' The school was then involved in the Technical and Vocational Education Initiative, and was experimenting with a modular curriculum.

In the expressive order, there was a less pronounced emphasis on discipline, which was much less obviously based on hierarchical control. Rather like St Hilda's at the other end of our status hierarchy, the prospectus referred to 'encouragement of self-discipline, tolerance, cooperation and mutual respect and the promotion of positive attitudes and values'. The lack of age- and sex-differentiating rituals was evident in flexible uniform requirements, which by comparison with Archbishop Ambrose were less restrictive and more open to individual interpretation. Regulation was largely confined to colour, ties were not required and students did not have to display their school affiliation outside through wearing blazers. In general, the school's openness to parents and the wider community was emphasized in its publicity.

These three examples illustrate the extent to which our schools vary not only in terms of sector, prestige and degree of selectivity, but also in organizational culture and ethos. These attributes all have a significant bearing on parents' choices and their children's subsequent experiences. In the next section we introduce the parents and outline the various ways in which they tried to ensure that their children embarked on secondary school careers that would help them to realize their academic promise.

Table 3.3 Occupational status of parents

	Fathers		Mothers	
	Frequency	Percentage	Frequency	Percentage
I: Professional	93	29.7	12	4.0
II: Managerial and technical	152	48.6	168	56.6
III NM: Skilled (non-manual)	24	7.7	88	29.6
III M: Skilled (manual)	37	11.8	14	4.7
IV: Partly skilled	5	1.6	14	4.7
V: Unskilled	2	0.6	1	0.3
Total	313	100.0	297	100.0

In the earlier study (Edwards *et al.* 1989), we used the Oxford Mobility Study scale to assign socio-economic status. In response to criticisms that this scale underrepresented the number of working-class pupils in the sample, we have used the OPCS (1991) scale in this book. An outline of the main classifications can be found in Appendix 2.

The table excludes those who were not in paid employment or whose occupational status is unknown. Of the fathers, under 1 per cent (3) were not in paid employment and we have no data for 9 per cent (31) of the sample. Of the mothers, 9 per cent (31) were not in any form of paid employment and there were no data for 6 per cent (19) of the sample.

The parents and their children

All of the children within our sample can be seen as potential recruits to the middle class. The majority came from middle-class homes themselves and all were deemed to be academically able with the prospect of gaining educational credentials that would open doors to middle-class occupations. The socio-economic profile of our respondents is outlined in Table 3.3.

Our informants had all been deemed academically able at the start of their secondary education. A majority had passed school entrance examinations at the age of 11, many for highly selective schools. The comprehensive school headteachers who had then identified our other informants as 'clearly of grammar school ability' may have defined that category differently in different localities, but they showed at interview a keen appreciation of which selective schools they were competing with for clever children and it was these that would have provided their frame of academic reference. They were certainly all within the 'top 20 per cent' ability band traditionally assumed to be 'naturally' equipped for selective schooling, higher education and high-status employment.

Given that all our children were academically able, a close relationship between parental occupations and school hierarchy might be expected. That is, it might be predicted that those with the highest socio-economic status would choose the most prestigious schools their children were 'qualified' to enter.

Choice of school, parental socio-economic status and parental education

At the start of this chapter, we mentioned changes in the educational land-scape within which school choices are made. It had certainly changed enough since the parents themselves were at school to make them unsure what new landmarks to look for, and to incline some towards the apparent safety of traditional selective provision. Greater scope for choosing away from the local school, and a wider range of alternatives, have since made choosing a school a more complicated process in urban areas than it was 20 years ago (Edwards *et al.* 1989: 184–213; David *et al.* 1994: 133–6). Even then, avoiding 'unsatisfactory' schools appeared to have been at least as influen-tial as positive preferences. While our cohort included many first-generation fee-payers, it did not show the pervasive middle-class 'decampment' to the private sector that we questioned in Chapter 2.

As Figure 3.2 shows, more parents in socio-economic groups I and II selected the most prestigious – the 'elite' and 'respectable' private – schools for their sons and daughters, they were also likely to send their children to schools that might be deemed at the lower end of our hierarchy of prestige – the state-maintained comprehensive schools.

In general, parents were more likely to send their children to private schools if they themselves had been to private schools. This applied to both mothers and fathers. The older established private schools were more likely to be used by privately educated parents than those schools that had recently been direct-grant schools and so partly inside the state sector (see Table 3.4).

If we look across the sample as a whole (Table 3.5), it is possible to recog-nize the characterization of two systems in which location is substantially

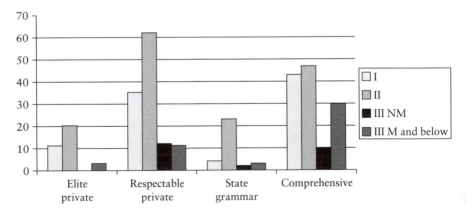

Figure 3.2 Rank of school and socio-economic status of parents (indicated by father's occupation)

Table 3.4   Proportions of parents who had been privately educated by school

	Percentage of fathers privately educated	Percentage of mothers privately educated
Cathedral College	83.3	66.7
St Hilda's	54.5	54.5
Bankside College	38.9	31.3
Dame Margaret's	30.4	39.1
Shirebrook	27.6	13.8
Highgrove County	25.0	0.0
Archbishop Ambrose	16.7	5.6
Nortown High	15.4	30.8
Vicarage Road	15.0	5.3
Milltown Grammar	15.0	5.0
Moorside	11.5	11.5
Parkside	11.1	0.0
Milltown High	4.2	3.8
Cherry Tree	3.4	0.0
Nortown Grammar	2.1	10.2
Rowton	0.0	0.0
Weston	0.0	14.3
Frampton	0.0	0.0

Excludes those parents who were schooled overseas or whose schooling is unknown.

Table 3.5   Proportions of parents who had been privately educated by sector

	Child's school type (%)	
	State	Private
Mother's school type		
State	57	43
Private[a]	20	80
Father's school type		
State	55	45
Private[a]	42	58

Excludes those parents who were schooled overseas or whose schooling is unknown.

[a]Includes direct-grant schools.

Table 3.6 Socio-economic background of students with assisted places (father's occupation)

	Frequency	Percentage
I	15	21.4
II	32	45.7
III NM	10	14.3
III M	10	14.3
IV	1	1.4
V	1	1.4
NIPE	1	1.4
Total	70	100.0
Missing data	14	

determined by birth, although the 'two nations' are not as separated educationally as sometimes claimed (Adonis and Pollard 1998).

There were, though, a small but significant number of parents from social class IV and lower whose children went to the more prestigious private schools. This is of course largely explained by the provision for 'poor but able' students made available by the Assisted Places Scheme (see Table 3.6). Although our own and other contemporary research suggested that the majority of place-holders were less 'needy' and less educationally disadvantaged than the scheme's advocates had intended or pretended, the few unambiguously working-class parents in our cohort who had sent their children to private schools had done so with its help (Tapper and Salter 1986; Papadakis and Taylor-Gooby 1987).

Recent research has identified parents who 'actively' choose a particular school, especially those who give priority to academic results, as likely to be middle class and relatively well educated (Adnett and Davies 2000). But it may be, and may have been in the 1980s, lower middle-class parents who are more likely to live in 'poor' areas with local schools they wish to escape (Hirsch 1997). In circumstances where academically selectively secondary education existed largely in the private sector, assisted places had special appeal for relatively impoverished or otherwise financially insecure middle-class families alert to a new opportunity to enhance the prospects of an able child. It was the conspicuous presence of many families of this kind that was a frequently cited finding from our original research.

Unsurprisingly, the full-fee-paying parents were generally of higher status. But contributing substantially to the absence of a clear linear relation between parent and school status is internal differentiation within the middle class. As might be expected from the 'scattering' of middle-class choices referred to in Chapter 2, but contrary to the 'mass decampment' thesis, a significant minority of class I parents had chosen to send their children to state-maintained comprehensives. Having described the schools in terms of different organizational cultures, we turn now to qualitative differences within our collection of middle-class parents.

Most classificatory systems differentiate vertically between upper and lower levels of occupational status, and we have noted relationships of that kind with the hierarchy of schools. Our interest here, however, is in *horizontal* distinctions within the broad grouping of 'middle class'. As mentioned in Chapter 1, the critical dividing lines have been contested, with the emphasis variously falling on fields of production (material and symbolic being a revised version of 'old' and 'new' middle class); sector of employment, whether public or private; and the asset basis of entrepreneurial, organizational and professional employment (Savage *et al.* 1992; Mann 1993). The divide between managerial and professional occupations is seen as especially significant because it is those working in the latter who are likely to rely most on cultural capital to secure or enhance their children's social position.

In categorizing our informants' family backgrounds, we have stayed with the convention of using father's occupation as the principal identifier. Although the mother's location may be more significant in relation to educational inheritance, the gendered nature of employment means that mother's occupation was less useful as a means of differentiation because the middle-class women were overwhelmingly employed in the public sector in professional positions, and were dependent on cultural rather than organizational or entrepreneurial assets (Table 3.7).

Our evidence shows no straightforward relationship between the kind of assets held and the kind of school selected. It is often claimed that it is easier for professionals to pass on their advantages (Fielding 1995), and we remarked in Chapter 2 on the past appeal of more academically oriented private schools to parents whose own occupational success had begun with

Table 3.7 Asset-based distribution of occupations (class III NM and above)

	Father		Mother	
	Frequency	*Percentage*	*Frequency*	*Percentage*
Professional	153	64	140	85
Managerial	79	33	22	13
Entrepreneurial	7	3	3	2
Total	239	100	165	100

We have omitted those individuals not in paid employment and those for whom no data were available or where the job descriptions were too vague to categorize.

Table 3.8 Sector of employment (class III NM and above)

	Father		Mother	
	Frequency	*Percentage*	*Frequency*	*Percentage*
Public	98	42	110	64
Private	130	56	59	34
Voluntary	5	2	3	2
Total	233	100	172	100

Again, as in Table 3.7, we have excluded parents not in paid employment, where there were missing data or where these were too vague to classify.

high-level qualifications. The relevance of sector of employment is attributed to whether economic and ideological support is derived from the state or the market, competition between them for resources and legitimacy in the provision of services producing different positionings for those working in each (Dunleavy 1980; Perkin 1989). In our cohort the middle-class fathers were divided fairly evenly between the two sectors; as already noted, the mothers were not (Table 3.8).

In relation to school choice, we might expect those working in the public sector to prefer maintained schools, and those in the private sector to prefer private schooling. Table 3.9 shows this to be the case.

We have also analysed our evidence in terms of the distinction between the 'old' middle class employed in the production and distribution of material goods and services, and the 'new' and rapidly expanding middle class engaged in the production, exploitation and distribution of symbolic knowledge (Table 3.10).

It is this distinction between the old and new middle class which Bernstein explored, and on which his analyses of social class and pedagogy are premised (Bernstein 1977, 1990, 1996). We draw heavily on that analysis in the rest of this chapter because it highlights significantly different orientations to family socialization and to formal schooling.

Choosing a secondary school

An overwhelming majority of our parents believed that educational success was crucial in determining their child's prospects, and that getting their child into the right kind of secondary school was crucial in bringing it about. There were wide differences, however, about what the 'right kind' of school looked like that can be related to tensions between the old and the new middle class.

Table 3.9 School sector and father's sector of employment

School sector	Father's sector of employment		
	Private	Public	Total
State			
Frequency (*n*)	41	82	123
% within school type	33	67	100
% within father's middle-class occupational sector	42	63	54
% of total	18	36	54
Private			
Frequency (*n*)	57	48	105
% within school type	54	46	100
% within father's middle-class occupational sector	58	37	46
% of total	25	21	46
Total			
Frequency (*n*)	98	130	228
% within school type	43	57	100
% within father's middle-class occupational sector	100	100	100
% of total	43	57	100

Table 3.10 Field of production (class III NM and above)

	Father		Mother	
	Frequency	*Percentage*	*Frequency*	*Percentage*
Symbolic	124	53	129	78
Material	109	47	37	22
Total	233	100	166	100

Drawing from Durkheim's work on the basis of social cohesion, Bernstein argued that contemporary society is underpinned not only by one form of organic solidarity but by two. Durkheim's own work concentrated on the form of solidarity which creates *individualism*. This is the form of solidarity developed by the old middle class and can be traced back to nineteenth-century values of enterprise and professional control. It is based upon what Bernstein (1977: 127) refers to as an 'ideology of radical individualism', which 'presupposes explicit and unambiguous values'. However, Bernstein argues that it is possible to identify a second form of organic solidarity that develops *personalized* identities and that has emerged rapidly in the past 50 years in line with the increasing emphasis on the creation and management of culture and communication. This is the form encouraged and reproduced by the new middle class in line with 'the scientific organization of work and corporate capitalism'.[1] In contrast to the ideology of radical individualism, personalized solidarity rests on implicit hierarchies and ambiguity.

Individualized and personalized identities are constituted through different socialization patterns, which Bernstein represents in terms of the strength of their boundary maintaining procedures. Old middle-class families tend to be *positional* in that 'boundary procedures are strong, the differentiation of members and the authority structure is based upon clear-cut, unambiguous definitions of the status of the member of the family' (Bernstein 1971: 184). This kind of family will emphasize the *individual*, leading to 'specific, unambiguous role identities and relatively inflexible role performances'. For the old middle class to reproduce individualized solidarity, 'variety must be severely reduced in order to ensure cultural reproduction' (Bernstein 1977: 125).

New middle-class families, on the other hand, tend to be *person-centred*, and 'boundary procedures are weak or flexible, the differentiation between members and the authority relationships are less on the basis of position . . . [and] more upon *differences between persons*' (Bernstein 1971: 184–5). The emphasis on the *person* leads to 'ambiguous personal identity and flexible role performances'. For the new middle class, 'variety must be encouraged to ensure interruption' (Bernstein 1977: 125).

From this perspective, old middle-class parents are likely to seek out schools where the instrumental and expressive orders are clearly bounded, closed and hierarchical. Archbishop Ambrose, as described above, is a school of that kind. New middle-class parents, in contrast, are more likely to select schools that are horizontally differentiated, and more open and inclusive in their organization and ethos (see Table 3.11). As Bernstein recognized, they might find them in the 'progressive' tradition of primary education, and then settle for more traditional provision at the secondary stage when they respond to the 'grim obduracy of the division of labour and of the narrow pathways to its positions of power and prestige' (Bernstein 1990: 126–7). Vicarage Road, as described above, was a secondary school with features that might appeal to the new middle class, but with the risks associated with its relative lack of a strong academic orientation.

With some exceptions, this tendency is evident in Table 3.11, with the comprehensive schools appealing to the new middle-class parents in our sample, and the grammar schools and 'respectable private' schools attracting old middle-class parents. We now explore the dispositions, values and dilemmas that lay behind these decisions. As in other publications from the research, we have used pseudonyms for individuals as well as schools.

Table 3.11   Schools selected by 'new' and 'old' middle-class parents (father's field of production, class III NM and above)

School	Percentage new middle class (n = 124)	Percentage old middle class (n = 109)
Frampton	88	13
Vicarage Road	85	15
Shirebrook	82	18
Cathedral College	80	20
Milltown Grammar	78	22
St Hilda's	71	29
Moorside	69	31
Highgrove County	63	38
Bankside College	54	46
Weston	50	50
Cherry Tree	47	53
Nortown Grammar	42	58
Nortown High	40	60
Milltown High	38	62
Parkside	38	63
Dame Margaret's	37	63
Archbishop Ambrose	23	77
Rowton	17	83
Overall distribution	53	47

'Old' middle-class parents

As Bernstein (1977: 124) noted, 'the ideologies of the old middle class were institutionalized in the public schools and through them into the grammar schools.' It is not surprising, then, that it was the schools which most resembled them – the former direct-grant and state-maintained grammar schools – that had been the main choice of our old middle-class families. They had not looked for educational innovation, but for academic selection and the attendant values of discipline and high achievement. The comments that follow are taken from parents at Milltown Grammar School for Boys.

> I like the discipline, the uniform, the orderliness.
>
> (Mrs Gold, bank official)

> The old methods – the three Rs are hard to beat.
>
> (Mrs Duncan, housewife, part-time secretary)

Mr Saddiqui, an accountant with a private company, had liked it as 'a quality school with discipline and a good record', and had disliked the relative inclusiveness of neighbouring comprehensive schools.

I don't want a school with many Pakistani children because of a predominant lack of interest in education . . . there are real problems of racial intolerance in some schools in Milltown. The problem is a lack of control and lack of discipline.

Preference for academic selection was often based on a belief that differences in ability were 'a fact of life' and that any attempt to think otherwise was not only misguided but potentially dangerous. Mrs Feenan, a housewife married to a biochemist, was typical in stating a scepticism about comprehensive education that the following comments also illustrate:

It doesn't seem to work. I have doubts about putting everyone in the same mould . . . because it ignores differences which are there. Comprehensive schools assume an unrealistic uniformity.

It's right that the bright kids be brought together and the not so bright. There's no alternative.

(Mrs Gold)

I don't like the idea of lumping bright children with not-so-bright; it holds bright kids back and doesn't help the not-so-bright . . . the problem with Labour Party policies is that they want to make everybody equal.

(Mrs Duncan)

Emphasis on individuality and individual effort was evident in many parents' perceptions of a selective school as more likely to reward academic merit, and to that extent as both better and fairer.

Everyone should have the chance to develop their own skills and personality as they can. But I don't believe in an ideal society. Nothing is perfect. Nothing is fair. I believe in individual opportunity and respect for individual difference . . . The development of him as a person is more important than the credentials, and the discipline, courtesy and old-fashioned standards. People seem to be looking for what is fast disappearing from the younger generation.

(Mrs Feenan)

It gives you standards to work with, and carry through to adult life.
(Mr Hemple, managing director of an old family firm)

And Mr Gold (investment advisor with a major bank) had wanted for his son

an education with discipline at its heart. It must start there . . . we are fully prepared to support the school in its demands, in behaviour and in learning, and assume those demands will be reasonable. We believe in living by the rules.

Old middle-class families are stereotypically more positional in their so-cial relations than new middle-class families. For instance, the emphasis on old-fashioned values also reflects a belief in a gendered division of labour. Although the following comment was of a kind heard only occasionally, even in positionally oriented families, it reflected a traditional view of the relative rates of return from educating sons compared with daughters. Mr Arniston justified sending his son to a selective private school and his daugh-ter to a comprehensive on the grounds that the boy would probably 'get married and have a wife and children' while the girl 'will probably have a husband to look after her'. In line with the more positional nature of old middle-class families, children often appeared to have little say in the choice of school, e.g.

It wasn't my choice. I didn't get a choice.

(Diane Webb, Nortown High)

I mean I don't feel like it was my decision. I feel it was like up to my Mum and Dad. Yeah I would've much preferred . . . and had my heart set on going [there]. I was very disappointed and I was the only girl from my junior school that went to Nortown High so that was completely terrifying.

(Lara Felton)

For some, progression had been made more likely by prior attendance at a private preparatory school, usually linked directly to the parents' pre-ferred secondary school, although there is enough evidence of switching sectors in both directions at that stage for this not to be taken for granted. Of those parents for whom the choice of a private school would have been new ground, some had sent their children to the comprehensive schools with reluctance. A few children had not passed the admissions test for their chosen private or grammar school even though they were considered by their teachers to be suitable candidates, or their parents had wanted pri-vate schooling but been unable to afford it. Mrs Goodlad (Shirebrook), who ran her own hairdressing business, recalled how she had been forced to withdraw her 'above average' son from a private primary school when her marriage fell apart, an event she also blamed for his subsequent failure to pass the entrance test to a nearby grammar school which had 'seemed to have better qualified teachers, more of an academic tradition and brought more pressure to do well'. Mrs Nightingale, married to the marketing director of a large building firm, supported the principle of 'parents' right to choose and to pay', which, she believed, led to 'the higher standards in uniform and manners – and the social selectiveness'. In the end, however, she and her husband had been persuaded by a visit and by the headteacher of the merits of Shirebrook.

The 'new' middle-class parents

Like their 'old' middle-class counterparts, the choices of 'new' middle-class parents scattered over all the schools in our sample. They were more likely, however, to favour those where the instrumental and expressive orders were differentiated and open, rather than hierarchical and closed. When they had chosen the latter, it was often reluctantly and with something of that 'deep-rooted ambivalence' that Bernstein identified as 'the ambience of this group':

> there are contradictions within personalized organic solidarity which create deeply felt ambiguities, as a consequence, the outcomes of the form of the socialization are less certain. The contemporary new middle class is unique, for in the socialization of its young is a sharp and penetrating contradiction between a subjective personal identity and an objective privatized identity; between the release of the person and the hierarchy of class.
>
> (Bernstein 1977: 136)

For those new middle-class parents with money and academically able children, and who lived within reach of elite schools, there were versions of private schooling that provided an acceptable way of reconciling their preference for personalized forms of education without risking academic success. Schools such as Cathedral College and St Hilda's had long-established 'liberal' reputations. Mrs Johnson, for example, a teacher, chose Cathedral College because it was academic and had this liberal tradition. Others, more often than not working in the public sector, had chosen a comprehensive school. That this had been an 'active' choice is evident from the fact that all of them had lived near fee-paying schools, and schools offering assisted places for which several would have been financially eligible. As Rhodes Boyson commented in his review of our earlier book, parents alert to the possibility of an assisted place, or who might otherwise have been ready to pay fees, were also likely to be 'parents wise enough to shop around' for an academically satisfactory comprehensive school (*Times Higher Education Supplement* 18 May 1990).

Values that resonated with some new middle-class parents were the very ones that old middle-class parents tended to eschew. For them the wider social and academic mix was a virtue rather than a flaw. They wanted, for example:

> more equal opportunities and the wider social mix, and the chance for the able children to realise that there's more to life than academic ability.
> (Mr Wellard, further education lecturer, Shirebrook)

> As parents of children who are doing well, it's fine. It's important for a child's education to come into contact with a wide range of backgrounds.
> (Dr and Mrs Reid, university lecturer and teacher, Shirebrook)

Dr Reid had felt 'seriously deprived' by his own private schooling of contact with children from a broad range of backgrounds, and had not wanted his children to suffer similarly.

Shirebrook exemplified in many ways the 'safe alternative' we have referred to. With a substantial middle-class intake and strong academic performance, it was not a school from which able children had to be 'rescued' by fee paying or by assisted places. Some parents at the school worried about comprehensives 'becoming increasingly difficult to work properly with all the cuts' (Mrs Steel, an NHS physiotherapist married to an NHS doctor), and that 'the cut-back in resources for state schools is worrying because some parents may feel tempted to buy their way out' (Mrs Bateman, married to a university professor). Mrs Charles, an ex-teacher married to an accountant, had initially secured a private school place for her son but had been 'put off' because it 'seemed too disciplined, too much imposed order, too much "we will shape them"'.

Both in the original pupil interviews and in our informants' recollections, children's own preferences had sometimes been decisive, perhaps reflecting the extent to which new middle-class parents value self-directedness over rule-boundedness. Bryan Modest (Vicarage Road) recalled: 'My wish was the sole deciding factor. I would have hated at that age, eleven years old, to be put somewhere away from a lot of people that I was like familiar with, which was my own concern.' Of course, in allowing their children to voice their preferences, some parents had already taken steps to ensure that the options were 'safe'. Several had moved house so as to be within the catchment of a favoured comprehensive. Thus Mrs Bateman (Shirebrook) reported that she and her husband had 'searched out the school first and then bought the house'. The Stillwells (teacher and university lecturer), then living in the nearby city, had entered their son for a private school to avoid the local comprehensive. Although he had passed the entry test, they had 'doubts about the fees and moved to Shirebrook partly with the school in mind'. Nigel Cormack's parents had moved into the catchment area of Cherry Tree Comprehensive, although he recalled his going there as

> entirely my choice – I think! From what I remember anyway. I can't remember the reasons really, but I presume it was because everyone else I knew was going there. One thing I do remember was being told, do you want to go to [a nearby private school] or do you want to do this. And I was given the choice.

Other parents had explored the credentials of local schools. Mrs Nightingale, for example, reported that her husband had asked Shirebrook's headteacher about the proportion of graduates on the staff, and Mrs Steel had established that 'clear streaming' ensured that 'the really able mix mainly with children of similar ability'.

For some parents, their final choice of a private school had come from a reluctant pragmatism rather than principle or family tradition.

> Comprehensive schools work better sometimes. I'm against academic selection – there wouldn't be any need if all comprehensives were good . . . Ideally, I wish you didn't have to make the choice.
>
> (Mr Irons, Indian doctor married to a nurse,
> Milltown Grammar)

> Comprehensives are on balance a better idea than the old grammar/secondary modern system . . . if it is organized properly, they are excellent. Some of the shire comprehensives were excellent.
>
> (Mr and Mrs Jaffe, both teachers in state schools,
> Milltown Grammar)

The Basseys (teacher and historian) sent their son to Cathedral College, despite being strongly pro-comprehensive 'in principle', because government had 'forced through the comprehensive system too soon, for example having to use split sites'. Like some other new middle-class parents, they thought that comprehensive schools were fine 'in other parts of Britain' (Mr Irons) or were 'disastrous' in inner-city areas, so that 'in Nortown you have to play the system' (Mr and Mrs Jaffe). Mrs Melrose and her husband had chosen Cathedral College despite declaring themselves against private schooling:

> I don't like private schools because they don't look at art and craft, yet local secondary schools were not good enough academically . . . Theoretically, I'm for comprehensives. I really would have liked to use a state school – they have a much more broad approach to knowledge.

Similarly, Mrs Parry remarked that 'state schools do a fantastic job', and was generally against academic selection because of its divisiveness, but when the time came 'local circumstances' led to the choice of Cathedral College. It was hard, as the Basseys put it, to argue against the statistic that 'at Cathedral College you have a 50 per cent chance of Oxbridge'.

Conclusion

In this chapter we have explored the diverse choices made by middle-class parents. Interviews with our informants, and with their parents some ten years or so earlier, indicated complex relationships and, sometimes, cross-cutting allegiances and preferences. Parents in some families had themselves been schooled in different sectors, or worked in different fields of production calling for different kinds of asset. Among the safest generalizations is that the most 'elite' members of the middle class chose the most elite schools, and that those in the lower socio-economic groups tended towards the lower end of the prestige hierarchy. But there was no simple linear relationship between socio-economic and school status. Horizontal divisions reflected different orientations towards learning and school organization, which Bernstein's distinction between old and new middle class helps us to understand. In general, the former tended to favour schools with the more hierarchical ethos found in state grammar schools and the 'respectable' private sector. New middle-class parents, more likely to favour more differentiation and openness, could find this both in elite schools and in some comprehensives. They were also more likely to have given weight to their child's preference. In the next three chapters, we follow their children's careers through school and examine how they responded to different school cultures, and the extent to which parents realized their hopes of aligning their own values with those of their chosen school.

Note

1 Of course, the new middle class itself is not homogeneous. There are elements within it that are ideologically predisposed towards traditional modes of education. Members of what Bernstein terms 'regulators' (the legal system, police, prison service, church), 'repairers' (medical/psychiatric services, social services) and 'executors' (civil service and bureaucrats) are likely to be more conservative than 'shapers' (creators of symbolic forms in arts and sciences), 'diffusers' (mass and specialized media) and 'reproducers' (teachers).

4 Success realized? Achievements at school

At the beginning of this book we questioned the common assumption, even within the sociology of education, that the close relationship between the middle classes and 'their' schools assures educational success. In Chapter 3 we identified variations in middle-class characteristics and allegiances, and cultural differences in the schools to which they send their children, which complicate the matching of family aspirations and school values. The educational careers that we analyse in the next chapters illustrate some of those complexities. The main heading of this chapter has a necessary question mark even though it is about a cohort more likely to succeed than to fail. Certainly if we locate our informants within the typologies employed in other concurrent research, most would be among the 'high-fliers' for whom academic credentials had represented the surest route to high-status employment, and their 'imagined futures' were largely constructed from the association of educational with occupational success (Biggart and Furlong 1996; Ball *et al.* 1999).

We begin by outlining their achievements at school, first in relation to national standards and then in relation to the three types of school they attended. The first task is easy because they are close contemporaries of the representative sample of young people included in the British Cohort Study (Bynner *et al.* 1997). By that comparison, the great majority had 'succeeded' at school. Compared with the national (English) figure of 30 per cent in 1988, 97 per cent achieved at least the 'threshold' qualification of five or more 'good' passes at O-level or GCSE. Whereas only 36 per cent in the Cohort Study had gained qualifications beyond that level, and only 21 per cent had graduated, our equivalent figures of 92 per cent and 76 per cent show very low rates of 'wastage' or of 'cooling out' from a cohort identified as academically promising at the outset of their secondary education (Power *et al.* 1999).

This general profile of relative success is not surprising, given our inform-ants' academic ability and predominantly middle-class backgrounds, and the privileged schooling that many of them had experienced. More interesting was whether those who had gone to private schools, and to academically selective schools in the private or public sectors, had been more successful in translating academic promise into educational achievement. Before report-ing our findings, we place them in the context of rapidly changing indica-tors of what counts as success.

Credential inflation

When Jackson and Marsden described the making of able working-class children into 'middle-class citizens', mere entry to a grammar school was usually enough to ensure at least white-collar employment for those who wanted it, even though about one in four of those formally identified as of grammar school ability failed to achieve the expected 'five good passes' at ordinary level. It was staying on into the sixth form, however, that they particularly associated with middle-class dominance of 'all the many avenues which open out' from that stage (Jackson and Marsden 1966: 25). This was far more likely to be regarded as a natural progression by middle-class families. Even in the mid-1980s about four in seven left full-time education, 'usually for good', at the age of 16. The age-participation rate in higher education was still only about one in eight, still below the 15 per cent level often taken as marking the boundary between 'elite' and 'mass' systems. Less than a decade later, 70 per cent were staying on at 16 and one in three was entering a university or college (Payne 1998). Our informants were therefore at school in the early stages of unprecedented growth in post-compulsory education, and in the attainment of 'advanced' qualifications. These changes, illustrated in Tables 4.1 and 4.2, were already making 'inter-mediate' credentials 'a declining asset' for the occupationally ambitious (Heath *et al.* 1992; Marshall *et al.* 1997).

The 'human capital' approach to 'investment' in extended education draws attention to how young people perceive the mechanisms through which edu-cational attainment translates into occupational success. The 'rationality' of their consequent decisions would seem to need some general knowledge of the relative status of occupations, and of the appropriate credentials to be considered for entry to a desired occupation or occupational level. Such

Table 4.1 Highest known educational qualifications of respondents and their parents

	Respondents		Fathers		Mothers	
	n	%	n	%	n	%
Up to O-level/GCSE	27	7.8	91	31.0	131	43.2
Up to A-level or equivalent	34	9.8	47	16.0	51	16.8
HE/FE equivalent	285	82.4	156	53.1	121	39.9
Total	346	100.0	294	100.0	303	100.0

Table 4.2 Respondents' social class and highest level of educational qualification

	GCSE (n = 26)	A-levels (n = 28)	HE (n = 211)
Class I (%)	0.0	2.9	97.1
Class II (%)	6.9	6.1	87.0
Class III NM (%)	14.9	34.0	51.1
Class III M (%)	50.0	20.0	30.0
Class IV (%)	50.0	0.0	50.0
Class V (%)	100.0	0.0	0.0

Excludes those with no paid employment.

'rational calculation' does not require them to believe that those credentials will provide knowledge and skills directly relevant to the employment they seek, 'only that private benefits follow from it' (Killeen *et al.* 1999: 113). As we illustrate in the chapters that follow, our respondents' 'calculations' included a keen appreciation of the benefits of 'good results' from 'good' or 'the best' universities.

The 'threshold' qualification and beyond

Five 'good passes' at the end of compulsory schooling had been the least expected of pupils 'of grammar school ability', even though many failed to achieve them. The survival of this prime indicator of 'effective' secondary school performance, and the consequent tendency to regard anything less as failure (Cockett and Callaghan 1996), might therefore appear a remarkable and anachronistic survival from the tripartite system. For many purposes, however, it has become a 'threshold' qualification. By the mid-1980s, when it was being taken almost for granted for the academically able, and achieved by about a third of the age-group, the private sector figure was already over 80 per cent (Payne 1998: 5). That it is now at or close to 100 per cent in many private schools appears to support Saunders' (1996: 69–70) conclusion that they have the capacity to protect even 'dull' (his word) middle-class children from downward mobility because 'they tend to do better than state schools at getting their children through examinations irrespective of their abilities or ambitions'.

For our 'clever' informants, the real tests therefore came at the next stage. At that time, staying on rates in private schools were already around 70 per cent. This compared not only with the 20 per cent in state schools but with around 50 per cent in the private sector 20 years earlier. The proportions of public school leavers with three A-level passes had risen from 20 to 45 per cent from 1961 to 1981, and the sector's share of 'high-flying' entrants to university was approaching 40 per cent (Halsey *et al.* 1984: 32–3). These figures illustrate both educational upgrading and levels with which state school pupils were competing. They also explain why the selection of credible schools for the allocation of assisted places had looked past O-level results to the range of A-level subjects available, results in those subjects and entry rates to higher education.

Staying on in full-time education was already therefore the 'obvious' decision for pupils who did well at 16. As national statistics showed for a slightly later period, it was taken by almost all those who had achieved high grades at GCSE and by no less than 98 per cent of those who had eight or more 'good passes' (Payne 1998: 22–3). Extending that route into higher education, and then into professional or managerial employment, had become the 'prime trajectory' for those able to take it (Banks *et al.* 1992). And although we have warned against exaggerating the smoothness of our respondents' progress, they were notably homogeneous in the educational choices they had made at, or in many cases some time before, the age of 16. They were certainly so by comparison with contemporaries deliberately chosen for their social and educational diversity, whose transitions into adult life had made 'easy generalisations impossible' (Ball *et al.* 1999). Not only did most of our respondents follow the 'prime trajectory', but very few had seriously considered doing anything else. Other forms of post-compulsory education and training were also emerging and expanding during the 1980s, although the unsuccessful challenge of the GNVQ to the dominance of A-levels was still several years away. But these alternatives were unfamiliar to young people, parents and employers alike, and their value in the employment market was unclear. Amid uncertainties intensified by the sharp decline in 'youth jobs', the A-level route had the advantages of being venerable, of being regularly extolled as the embodiment of traditional academic standards, and of offering prospects of good jobs through well defined educational stages (Edwards 1997).

If 'almost any collection of A-levels' was preferable to vocational 'equivalents' (Killeen *et al.* 1999), this was a realistic assessment of the preferences of employers as well as universities. It reflected the continuing absence of 'different but equal' technical routes of the kind available (for example) in Germany. Grammar schools and the more 'academic' private schools were very unlikely to offer any alternative, 'abler' comprehensive school pupils were unlikely to seek one, and students following vocationally 'equivalent' routes are almost entirely missing from our data. As with the sharply decreasing proportions of high socio-economic status students in the general, technical and vocational tracks in French secondary education, this suggests 'a positional rather than a pedagogical logic' (Duru-Bellat 2000). Media highlighting of high average A-level scores as indicating a school's academic excellence also gave the private sector a vested interest in preserving that examination in its traditional form, as the first chief executive of the National Curriculum Council noted regretfully when explaining the failure of successive efforts to broaden and modernize it (Graham 1993). The relative superiority of private schools has been reduced since the 1980s because the *rate* of improvement by state schools has been greater (Gorard 2000), and a difference in average points leaves enough room for variation and overlap around them to undermine over-generalized claims to private sector superiority. Nevertheless, as a more recent sector-level generalization, schools that contain 8 per cent of pupils of compulsory school age now produce 22 per cent of A-level entries, 30 per cent of those gaining three or more A-grades and over 40 per cent of passes in the 'hardest' subjects of physics, mathematics and economics (*Times Educational Supplement* 7 July 2000).

That the A-level has remained primarily a strongly classified subject examination, dominated by largely the same 'academic' subjects as a generation or even two generations ago, may seem to support complaints about the economic irrelevance of the traditional liberal curriculum. Such complaints tend to underestimate both its historical significance in marking *social* distinction and its continued market value for employment in an economy dominated not by manufacturing but by financial and related services. What is certainly the case is that this is the curriculum regarded as suitable training for future leaders. As we note in Chapter 7, what Bernstein described as the 'regionalization' of knowledge into areas that blur or even remove traditional academic boundaries has become increasingly apparent in higher education. But at school level, such 'integration', and the emphasis on 'applicability' that commonly accompanies it, remain confined largely to the less academically and occupationally 'promising'. For the 'academically able' and especially those in elite secondary education, knowledge continues to be transmitted through 'hierarchically ordered, strongly bounded, explicitly stratified and sequenced pedagogic discourses and practices' (Bernstein 1999: 248–51).

Relative success

Summarizing an interim report of our findings, the *Economist* (25 April 1998) reported simply that those who had gone to fee-paying schools 'did better at A-level, went on to the most prestigious universities, and ended up in the best jobs'. A causal sequence was implied: namely, that the 'best' A-level results justified entry to the 'best' universities, where further success justified access to the 'best' jobs. This might be interpreted as supporting the meritocratic proposition that whatever the inequalities of the past, what matters now is not social class 'but whether you are bright and whether you worked hard' (Saunders 1996: 72). However, the *Economist* summary might instead seem to support the conclusion that while the labour market has become more meritocratic in its greater reliance on accredited academic achievement, many middle-class families have continued to find privileged routes to the most marketable education credentials.

Table 4.3 appears to indicate significant relative advantage. It also seems to illustrate how far the 'academic revolution' mentioned in our opening chapter had transformed the private sector in a few decades from 'a disparate and vulnerable collection of institutions' into a 'fairly unified structure of four hundred private meritocratic academies' (Adonis and Pollard 1998: 43). That generalization typically ignores the sector's less exalted reaches, but the schools our respondents attended were certainly among the high performers.

Table 4.3 Distribution (percentages) of A-level points by school sector

	All respondents		Those with A-levels	
	Private (n = 174)	State (n = 170)	Private (n = 164)	State (n = 146)
0–9	8.6	32.4	3.0	21.2
10–19	24.1	25.3	25.6	29.5
20–29	42.0	34.1	44.5	39.7
30+	25.3	8.2	26.8	9.6

A-level General Studies taken as an additional A-level in many private schools has been excluded from all statistics relating to the number or points scores of A-levels achieved.

The mean score for those pupils who obtained their A-levels in private schools was 23.1, compared with 17.6 in the state sector (16.5 with the grammar school pupils excluded). Overall points scores can be a misleading comparator because they obviously advantage schools, most often private schools for boys, whose students commonly take four rather than three subjects. But in our data, mean scores per subject showed similar if rather smaller differences. The mean subject grade for our privately schooled informants was 7.7, just below a B grade, compared with 7.2 for those from grammar schools and 6.5, just over a C grade, for those from comprehensive schools. Where competition for places at prestigious universities is most severe, even small differences between applicants, or between required and actual grades, can be decisive.

There were significant gender differences in attainment. We explore these in some detail, partly because our respondents were reaching the end of their school careers at about the time girls' academic performance was catching up, and about to overtake, that of boys. It is also because the girls' private schools in our study were conspicuous examples of the 'education feminism' referred to earlier.

That all our private schools were single-sex and all but one of the comprehensive schools coeducational makes it impossible to comment on the benefits or otherwise of single-sex schooling, a matter that educational league tables have highlighted because they tend to show a large number of 'top places' being taken by single-sex schools from the public and private sectors. That these are more often girls' schools has prompted suggestions that girls benefit especially from single sex schooling, a possibility that several of the schools in our study had explicitly indicated. Finally, as we discuss more fully in Chapter 9, professions requiring graduate qualifications have been both the fastest growing sector of employment and the sector in which female participation grew faster than male (Crompton 1992; Egerton 1997). The relative advantage enjoyed by better qualified over less well qualified women in the labour market has become greater than the equivalent gap for men. This was evident in our study.

As in more recent research (Arnot et al. 1999), female students had done rather better at A-level, with 89 per cent achieving at least two A-level passes compared with 86 per cent of males, with a larger gap (80 and 73 per cent) in those getting graduate qualifications. However, when we begin to look within school sectors, the picture becomes more complicated. In the private sector, the gender gap was wider. Of those who had been to private schools, relatively more girls than boys obtained at least two A-level passes (99 compared with 89 per cent), completed a degree (92 against 73 per cent) and were taking or had already completed a higher degree (12 against 9 per cent). Moreover, there was greater polarization of educational performance among the males, which was especially marked in the single-sex, academically selective schools, both private and public. In those schools, the mean A-level score of female pupils was two points higher than that of the males from similar schools, and the range of pupil performance was markedly smaller. Among those educated at comprehensive schools, the picture of male and female attainment was reversed. Girls did marginally less well than boys, and their range of performance was somewhat greater.

Although academic selection is still quite closely associated with single-sex schooling, the fact that all our coeducational schools were comprehensive

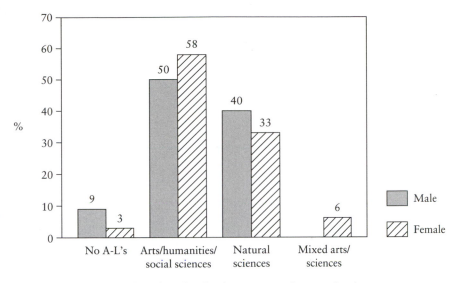

Figure 4.1   Male and female A-level subjects in single-sex schools

made it impossible to consider that factor separately. We did take into account, however, the overt commitment of the girls' selective schools to encouraging their pupils to reject all gender categorizing of 'appropriate' subjects to study or occupations to enter. Several of them were reported at interview to have placed particular emphasis on high achievements in science as a critical arena for challenging male dominance, and resembled that combination of 'academicism and modernism' described by Ball and Gewirtz (1997). In general, however, our evidence showed the predictable gender gap in choice of A-level subjects, with male students more often favouring predominantly science subjects and female students favouring arts and humanities. As Figures 4.1 and 4.2 show, however, the gap was significantly wider for students at coeducational schools. It virtually disappeared in the two state grammar schools.

Complex interaction between gender and school type draws attention to differences between individual institutions. The *Economist*'s generalizations ignored within-sector variation, which our findings showed to be as large as variation between sectors. Overall, our informants from two of the comprehensive schools had done better than those from two of the private schools and one of the grammar schools. There was also a difference of nearly 20 points in the average scores of the nine private schools compared with ten between the comprehensive school averages. There is no doubt, however, that even small differences in A-level grades produced significantly different opportunities for translating school achievements into high-status university places. We explore these in Chapters 7 and 9, because they suggest a significant private schooling advantage. In the next chapter, we

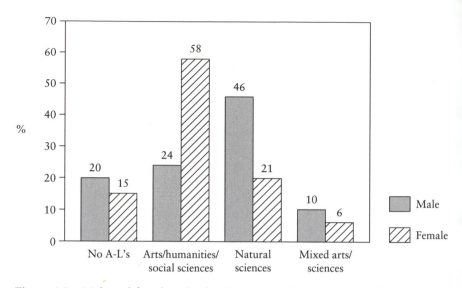

Figure 4.2 Male and female A-level subjects in coeducational schools

examine the extent to which comprehensive school cultures, which we have characterized as relatively open, differentiated and inclusive, and private and selective school cultures, which we characterized as tending towards closure and stratification, facilitated or hindered the educational and social progress of our informants.

5 Fitting in and getting on

I wish Milltown Boys' was still as good as when I was there.

I wish Milltown Boys' had burned down to the ground while I watched.

What is it that makes two young people looking back at their shared years at the same school have such different feelings? In this chapter we explore students' various experiences of the different schools they attended in order to unravel the complex relationship between the culture of the home and the culture of the school.

In their thinking about the 'right' school for their children, parents expressed a range of concerns about the options they saw as available. There was a common concern that their children should be 'happy' and 'successful' at school, but there were some clear differences about what might contribute to this. Many of those middle-class parents who had ideological preferences for comprehensive education valued the social dimensions, but expressed anxieties that their academically able children might fall into the 'wrong crowd', that they might not be 'stretched' sufficiently, or even that they might be isolated and stigmatized as being 'too clever'. Not surprisingly, these concerns were less frequently cited by those parents who chose selective schools, particularly in the private sector. They felt that academic and financial exclusivity would 'safeguard' their children from what they saw as 'unsavoury' elements and guarantee an environment in which academic success would be encouraged and celebrated. However, they too had

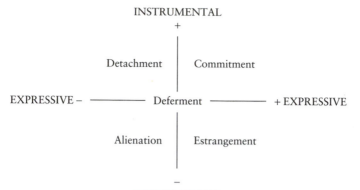

INSTRUMENTAL
+

Detachment | Commitment

EXPRESSIVE – ——— Deferment ——— + EXPRESSIVE

Alienation | Estrangement

–
INSTRUMENTAL

Figure 5.1 Types of involvement in the role of the pupil (after Bernstein 1977: 50)

concerns, particularly about whether their children would 'cope' and whether they would 'fit in'.

'Fitting in' can take a variety of forms. Bernstein (1977) outlines five potential relationships that pupils can develop towards their schooling: commitment, alienation, detachment, estrangement and deferment (see Figure 5.1). The positions of commitment and alienation need the least explaining – indeed, these are often the only positions given serious attention in some research (e.g. Willis 1977; Corrigan 1979). Bernstein's three further types of involvement offer the potential for more subtle analysis. Detachment arises when the pupil both understands and accepts the instrumental order but rejects the expressive order of the school. Conversely, estrangement occurs when the pupil understands and accepts the expressive order and also accepts the ends of the instrumental order but fails to understand the means. Deferment is when the pupil's involvement is suspended – 'watching the state of play' (Bernstein 1977: 45).[1]

There are strong parallels here between Bernstein's categories and those developed by Wakeford (1969) and Woods (1977), who draw on Merton's (1957) schema designed to understand the relationship between institutional culture and individual behaviour. However, while Woods's adaptation has the advantage of providing a wider range of possibilities *within* each position (for instance, he identifies a number of variants of 'conformity'), he does not provide a means of distinguishing between school types. Certainly for our research, given the wide variety of markedly different institutions with which we are dealing, classification of school cultures has been a starting point in the analysis. We have reported elsewhere (Power *et al.* 1998b) how the relationship between the culture of the school and the culture of the family contributed to contrasting modes of involvement between students at Archbishop Ambrose and Vicarage Road. In this chapter, we explore in more detail students' relationship with their school in terms of their sense of belonging, their academic identity and their relations with their peers, and how these relationships are influenced by school type. In the next chapter we examine the extent to which these experiences are gendered.

Finding one's place

Many of our respondents remember being anxious about their transition to secondary school. However, such fears were recalled less vividly by those students who went to comprehensive schools, partly because they were far more likely to progress to secondary school with fellow primary school classmates. It is also the case that these schools did not deliberately attempt to insulate their pupils from 'neighbourhood influences' or create that 'closed' and hierarchical structure that, as we saw in Chapter 3, characterized both of the state grammar schools and many of the private schools. These degrees of openness and closure created different experiences and challenges for our students as they struggled to 'fit in' academically and socially.

Selective schooling: making the grade

The trauma of starting secondary school is keenly remembered by those entering academically selective schools. The majority (68 per cent of those in the private schools and 77 per cent of those in the state grammar schools) of our students transferred from state primary schools and were confronted by a school culture that was very different in terms of its academic profile, demands and disciplinary practices.

The overall ethos of their new schools seemed to many to be very different. If state-maintained primary schools can be characterized in terms of strong expressive and weaker instrumental orders, schools such as Archbishop Ambrose provide strong instrumental and weaker expressive orders – with the latter being marked by hierarchy rather than differentiation. As Adrian Slocombe recalls of Archbishop Ambrose:

> It was a daunting old school, with archaic practices and prefects, different colour gowns, pictures of dead headmasters from years back on the assembly walls, panelled over walls. The whole thing is steeped in history because it was an old school. It wasn't anything like I expected and it was really daunting at eleven years old. You're just a sort of little kid and there are these six foot giants who were prefects who spent years apart and when you become sixteen years old, your perception changes and when you look at first years and think 'god were we like that?' When we were eleven, it was just incredible. So, yes it

was difficult, it wasn't friendly, it wasn't that easy to fit in. It was very traditional and I think they still had the cane when I started there and it was there for only a year or two and the headmaster was a proper old school headmaster. It was like I imagine Oxford or Cambridge to be – the old dons and fellows.

Many students also faced new subjects and disciplinary practices:

When I started, one of the first lessons I had was Latin and I was one of the few people, but there must have been perhaps half a dozen people out of 30, who'd not been to a prep school. That might not be right but it certainly felt that way. And quite a lot of the people in the school knew each other from prep school, or they even knew people from other prep schools or they knew people through their parents, and in Latin I was one of the very few people in the room who'd not actually done any Latin before. I was quite surprised that I was going to have to catch up with these people.

(Hugh Durack, Nortown Grammar)

I found the discipline very, very difficult because it was a very, well I mean I considered it after junior school, very disciplined, and that was really hard to come to terms with in terms of presentation, school uniform and the whole idea of like we had to, there was a downstairs and upstairs, there were two stairs at each end of the school and if you went up the downstairs or down the upstairs you know, you were penalized and I remember that being really difficult to adjust to.

(Lara Felton, Milltown High)

Although students transferring to comprehensive schools also faced new cultures, subjects and homework demands, the contrasts between the instrumental and expressive orders of their primary and secondary schools were less marked. In addition, the move between schools was usually experienced collectively as groups of children moved up together from one school to the next. In some of our private schools, those transferring from state-maintained primary schools often felt in the minority. As Hugh Durack (Nortown Grammar) recalls:

There was a bit of bullying to start with basically because a lot of the kids there had had the experience of bells going off at the end of lessons and standing up when the teacher comes into the room and calling everybody 'sir' and wearing a uniform all the time, and some of the academic subjects as well which I hadn't had. And so the first six months or so I had some difficulty fitting in. The other thing was homework. They'd all done homework and I'd never done any homework in my life apart from the tutoring to get into school. It wasn't something that happened at primary school.

55

However, it is the sense of fitting into the academic hierarchy that is most strongly remembered. Our young people had often been considered among the most able at their primary schools. The sense of their own abilities often underwent a painful reappraisal when they joined the secondary school.

> I was above average, but I wasn't top of the class, and that didn't help, because whereas at junior school I'd always come out top, I didn't like . . . it's the old syndrome of big fish in small pond moving to a . . . just sort of above average, and I'm quite competitive, and I wasn't quite so keen on that, you know.
>
> (Leah Tucker, Dame Margaret's)

> Everybody had come from being top of their primary school; I can remember some lads being called thick by other pupils. There was a bit of elitism about the three fast sets; even within the fast sets there was elitism in that the people at the bottom of the fast sets were regarded as dodos.
>
> (Irving Bungay, Nortown Grammar)

It is difficult to exaggerate the extent to which academic hierarchy features in their accounts of their identity within the school. Many students displayed an acute sense of where they were relative to their peers:

> In the top 10 per cent perhaps. I mean there were people that were certainly brighter than I was but they were exceptional. I was in the sort of next band down from that.
>
> (Cate Bozza, St Hilda's)

> I feel quite sad when I look back, because in my primary school I was always at the top, and I did very well in these entrance exams, and I had always been told that I was very bright, and I knew I was. I always did very well and I found work very very easy. I had no problems. Then I came to Dame Margaret's High School, I was talking about this to this girl that I'm still very friendly with, and I just foundered at Dame Margaret's High School, because there were so many bright people, I became just average.
>
> (Naomi Chandler, Dame Margaret's)

Sometimes pupils were quite literally 'ranked':

> First two years I was sort of just below the middle mark of the class, I suppose, in most subjects. And we got grades every half term and those grades were very heavily weighted towards . . . it's the sort of zero, zero is the null point and the vast majority of people got way above. Only a few people got below it and I was just sort of, hovering just above it which although it was just above zero, I still felt that I was not performing to scratch.
>
> (Andrew Rider, Nortown Grammar)

We have written elsewhere (Power *et al.* 1998a) of the problems of being seen as 'average' and 'mediocre' in highly pressured academic environments – as we discuss in the next chapter, this seemed to be particularly an issue for boys. In general, though, students at our private schools were more worried about their academic progress than were their counterparts at comprehensive schools.

For some students, the pressure facilitated their progress. It seemed to provide a totalizing environment, where it was easier to go with the grain than against it. Schools like Nortown Grammar seemed particularly strong in this dimension.

> People that basically get on, proactive people, I would say, there were quite a lot of people like me who were just not pulling their weight, for various reasons, but if you had the motivation, they would have basically channelled you through, and shepherded you along, and you would have done very well.
>
> (Daniel Brighten, Nortown Grammar)

When students appear to have accepted the ends and means of schools such as these, *and* been able to do the work, they become 'committed' (Bernstein 1977) to the culture and organization of the school. However, for others, it had been demotivating. Indeed, some never seemed fully to recover from the loss of confidence they experienced at the start of their secondary school careers. There are certainly higher proportions of students who went to private schools who can be identified as 'alienated' or 'estranged' (Bernstein 1977) when they talk about their involvement with their school. The pressure to achieve could lead to students becoming antagonistic towards their school. Although these shared the values of the school, they did not have the means to succeed – because of the heavy academic demands of such an academically oriented school and/or inappropriate cultural resources within the home. As Bernstein (1977: 46) notes, 'the blighted aspirations, combined with a low stream, coupled with his loyalty to the school, may make his school experience particularly painful and damaging.' Although it is possible to speculate that a position of commitment to the school may be engineered through the expressive order, this is problematic in a school in which the stratification of pupils by academic achievement is so visible. Far from encouraging these students to work harder, the strong sense of inferiority that such visible hierarchy engendered could serve to sap confidence.

> As soon as I went to Dame Margaret's, I mean, I basically didn't speak for a year and a half. I was really quiet. I went sort of very much, you know, inside myself. I mean I used to be the narrator for the school plays at primary school and I used to stand up in front of everybody, chat-chat-chat. There I couldn't even read aloud in an English lesson

from a book without kind of getting really nervous and stuttering and all the rest of it, so my confidence just kind of went.

(Celia Fyfe, Dame Margaret's)

The school wasn't a good confidence builder because of the platform from which people had come into Nortown Grammar School. I think it's a very hard situation if you have been used to being top and suddenly you're no longer top, and if you've always been told how wonderful you are and suddenly you're being told how hopeless you are.

(Irving Bungay, Nortown Grammar)

As we explore more fully in Chapter 8, some of those respondents who left selective schools with qualifications that were significantly superior to their age cohort at other schools describe their school careers in terms of 'disappointment' and 'failure':

I didn't really get any attention, because at Dame Margaret's High School they concentrated sort of mainly on the top bracket and I didn't really do particularly well. I know it looks as though I did from my O-levels, but with my A-levels I did badly, I know, so I didn't really feel that bright.

(Naomi Chandler, Dame Margaret's)

Private schools appear better in terms of academic results; but in my experience my personal confidence at the time that I left Nortown Grammar School was at an all time low.

(Irving Bungay, Nortown Grammar)

Some accounts give the impression of an academic treadmill that was hard to get back on once you'd slipped off:

People develop at different rates. I think that I developed quite early but then went through my lax period in my early teens. In the environment that they foster, there's no contingency plan if you take your foot off the gas. There's no way to pick people back up.

(Irving Bungay, Nortown Grammar)

The need to find a niche for oneself in these highly pressured academic environments required not just fitting in academically but also fitting in socially. In general, within-school social networks were very important to students at private schools and there was less emphasis on spending time together with 'out of school' friends (see Table 5.1).

Going to a private school also created significant divisions between social lives at home and school. In part this was because of the longer distances between home and school and the greater number of extra-curricular activities, but it was also because these pupils tended to inhabit two different social worlds. Several reported difficulties in maintaining friendships with

Table 5.1 To what extent was spending time together out of school with friends important?

	Private (%)	Comprehensive (%)	Total (%)
Was not important	26.9 (n = 47)	15.3 (n = 21)	21.8 (n = 68)
Was quite important	38.3 (n = 67)	39.4 (n = 54)	38.8 (n = 121)
Was very important	34.9 (n = 61)	45.3 (n = 62)	39.4 (n = 123)

their local friends who had gone on to state-maintained schools. They variously remembered being accused of going to 'snobby' schools:

> There were some people there and often they're faced with the idea in people's minds that if you were rich you could send your kids to Nortown Grammar School, whether they were clever or not; which is absolutely not the case. So I had to fight a lot of that sort of attitude from my peer group outside school. They thought I was being snobby and that my family was being snobby and I was going to a posh school. And I was like, 'No I'm not going to a posh school; I'm just going to a different school.'
>
> (Stephen Holloway, Nortown Grammar)

> It opens you up to a bit of stick, basically, not from your friends, but like friends of theirs that don't know you. You know it's a very lah-di-dah attitude, sort of inverted snobbery really, that's what it was.
>
> (Daniel Brighten, Nortown Grammar)

The strength of the antipathy between comprehensive and selective schools is very evident in accounts from students attending all types of schools:

> All my friends from primary school ignored me. They thought that I turned into this snob because I'd gone to the posh school; that was quite difficult.
>
> (Sadie Wiggin, Dame Margaret's)

> And I think again quite a lot of snobbery on both parts and they would shout and call us names and we'd just think toe-rags from down the road. And there was very much different, we didn't mix at all with them.
>
> (Naomi Sharples, Dame Margaret's)

> If there had been a situation where we were all waiting for the bus together or something like that, then there would have been problems, but they used to get a different bus, so we just didn't see them. You'd occasionally get, if you walked past them and you happened to have your school blazer on, you'd get 'Oh, look at the snob and look at the swot.'
>
> (Peta Roper, Highgrove County)

For those in the comprehensive schools such as Vicarage Road, private school students in particular were seen to be alien:

> The general perception was that everyone in Clifton Grammar was queer – it was queer, snobby, or rich . . . They probably thought of us as scum of the earth.
>
> (William Jowitt, Vicarage Road)

> I mean Dame Margaret's it was like oh they're all a bunch of snobs.
>
> (Chloe Carter, Vicarage Road)

> That seemed a very snooty sort of school because we heard rumours for example that they weren't allowed to talk on the ground floor, although I'm sure they were all Chinese whispers but we all, we just couldn't quite fathom that out really and they obviously thought that was a real military like school . . . a really intelligent, bright sort of school.
>
> (Graham Chambers, Vicarage Road)

Comprehensive schooling: an inclusive culture?

There are certainly differences between the accounts of our comprehensive school pupils and those of our private and grammar school pupils. Those who attended comprehensive schools rarely recalled difficulties with settling in, and fewer had what might be called 'damaged' academic identities. There were lower levels of 'alienation', and certainly fewer examples of 'estrangement'. If students were not committed to their schools, they were more likely to be 'detached' (Bernstein 1977). Although the majority (70 per cent) of our young people said that they were 'happy at school', those who recalled being 'not happy' at school were more often those who went to private schools.

Many of our ex-comprehensive school respondents are clearly 'committed' to the comprehensive experience. Patrick Welcome (Moorside), for instance, speaks warmly of the way in which his school gave him social confidence:

> One thing that I got from Moorside, was an ability to mix and talk to people. I communicate with everybody which is such a big asset nowadays. I have no qualms about talking to anybody . . . I think that was something that I got from the school, partly my parents as well, but I think I was quite active at school and the school encouraged you to be active.

It would be easy to romanticize comprehensive schools as providing environments where *all* pupils can fit in and where social networks cross class and cultural boundaries. Such a view would be unrealistic, however. Within the comprehensive school, our students recalled moving in fairly narrow circles. In some cases these were determined by streaming and subject setting.

> We were grouped according to ability in some of the classes but not all because there were so few people. For example, my Spanish class, there was just one class, one group who took Spanish GCSE and they were I'd say 50 per cent of the class didn't want to learn. So the teacher, I mean she told me that she aimed to teach the 50 per cent that wanted to learn and . . . to teach the higher levels.
>
> (Bernadette Glassford, Vicarage Road)

As Ford (1969) has argued, comprehensive schools can lead to more exclusive social class grouping within schools than selective schools. Our respondents' accounts illustrate the extent to which there were informal divisions and ranking as our students settled into academic and social circles of 'people like us':

> I remember at school, three of my class and one other chap sat with me. In all my classes. We used to hang around together outside classes as well in classes and he was of equal sort of status. We did used to hang around and there was the obviously the much more brainier people that you see, who you quite associate with further upper class and then there'd be pupils a little less brainier and you look at them maybe a bit further down . . . Because of the catchment obviously you get very, loads of different social classes from poor people right through to probably quite wealthy people who just didn't want to send their kids to a private school or whatever and there was a definite trend, you can see people . . . from the poorer backgrounds or the less privileged backgrounds would definitely fall into the lower categories . . . So we had a definitely, definitely a sort of banding social scale.
>
> (Bryan Modest, Vicarage Road)

> The crowd I knocked around with were quite into the school and things. But there were a lot obviously who weren't interested at all and used to spoil things in class . . . You just got on with your work and ignored them.
>
> (Catherine Brunning, Rowton)

> There was definite groups and there was mainly the, as they probably would take it, the well spoken and the average person and there was a big divide between that, there was nothing in the middle. There was no animosity between it but you could always feel there was a group of people here and a group of people there. I remember in the first couple of years I was always being called a snob or whatever, I spoke differ-ent to they did . . . most of my friends tended to speak the same as me

anyway, so . . . I don't think it was snobbish but it wasn't . . . you don't want to use common, but it wasn't slang.

(William Jowitt, Vicarage Road)

The people I was friends with who were involved in music did seem to be from the top streams, but that was probably because I knew them anyway and then we were involved in something outside the classes as well. I don't know; I think there was probably a mix, but I don't know.

(Amelia Otis, Parkside)

Although students speak positively of the breadth of social intake, it tends to be in terms of 'meeting' people from other backgrounds rather than integrating or becoming 'friends' with them:

But having said that it was really good because there was a real, not a total, but quite a cross-section of society and I met a lot of people, all sorts of people, that I think it's good because you learn to get along with a lot of these people.

(Chloe Carter, Vicarage Road)

It is worth noting that our comprehensive school students were *more* likely to be anxious about being 'made fun of' or being 'called names' (see Tables 5.2 and 5.3).

Despite many comments from our ex-comprehensive school respondents about 'taking the rough with the smooth', 'mixing with all types', some of our respondents do remember being isolated:

Table 5.2 To what extent were you worried about other pupils making fun of you?

	Private	Comprehensive	Total
Never worried you (%)	44.6 (*n* = 78)	31.2 (*n* = 43)	38.7 (*n* = 121)
Worried you a little (%)	37.7 (*n* = 66)	49.3 (*n* = 68)	42.8 (*n* = 134)
Worried you a lot (%)	17.7 (*n* = 31)	19.6 (*n* = 27)	18.5 (*n* = 58)

Table 5.3 To what extent were you worried about being called names?

	Private	Comprehensive	Total
Never worried you (%)	59.4 (*n* = 104)	44.2 (*n* = 61)	52.7 (*n* = 165)
Worried you a little (%)	29.7 (*n* = 52)	43.5 (*n* = 60)	35.8 (*n* = 112)
Worried you a lot (%)	10.9 (*n* = 19)	12.3 (*n* = 17)	11.5 (*n* = 36)

> I came from a run-down area on the other side of Nortown. I found
> myself suddenly in this sort of, odd little valley, that would like to
> think it was still Yorkshire, where quite a lot of the people had been
> there for three generations and those that haven't are the hated
> comers-in and there are all sorts of local tribalisms and snobberies
> like that . . . these kinds of people that gave me such a hard time.
>
> (Sian Allan, Moorside)

And despite the inclusive rhetoric of comprehensive education, these schools
do not appear to have been particularly inclusive towards the few black
and Asian students in our sample:

> Especially in Vicarage Road, I found that people in that sort of area
> are a bit more, shall we say bigoted in their, even like obviously it must
> be the parents because it comes down through the kids and they're a
> bit more racist and things like that and pick on kids from different
> countries and things who are not the same colour as them and I
> remember in certain tutorial groups where, I don't look Pakistani
> really to some people, and so a lot of comments that were made in the
> religious studies group were made at foreign people without these
> people realizing where I was from and things . . . From talking to my
> friends, a lot of my friends who are Asian, I don't think people realize
> how much persecution there is in schools.
>
> (Mark Saheed, Vicarage Road)

Mark Saheed moved from Vicarage Road and went to the neighbouring
private school for his sixth form, an environment he found more comfortable:

> I think I got on better and had more in common with the people at
> Clifton Grammar than I did with the people at Vicarage Road . . . I'd
> say I felt more comfortable with the people at Clifton Grammar because
> they were more similar to me than the people at Vicarage Road . . . the
> people at Clifton Grammar, they had similar backgrounds to me, they
> had similar parents, some of them were Asian, and so it was a much
> more mixed group of people who got on together and it seems to me
> that you, at least at Clifton Grammar you could keep a little bit more
> of your own identity than you could at Vicarage Road because you
> had to basically assimilate a little bit more I think at Vicarage Road
> than you did at Clifton.

Of course, this shift may be connected with the transfer to sixth form, not
just the transfer to private schools. For many of our students, their sixth
form years felt qualitatively different and marked a significant change in
relationships with other pupils and with teachers in particular, at both
private and state schools. This shift may be connected with leaving behind
adolescence, a key aspect of which is the development of appropriate sexual

identities. Involvement at school – with classmates and teachers – is also highly gendered. In the next chapter, we examine some of the ways in which the different types of schooling variously fostered and hindered the development of particular forms of gendered identities that themselves either facilitated or impeded academic progress.

Note

1 This position is of only passing interest to us here, given the longitudinal and retrospective nature of our respondents' biographies and the temporary nature of deferment.

Schoolgirls, schoolboys
and school work

During the 1970s, 1980s and 1990s, research in the sociology of education began to throw light on the relationship between schooling, gender and sexuality (Connell 1989, 1996; Mac an Ghaill 1994; Epstein and Johnson 1998).

Early research in this area usually addressed the issue of how schools limited girls' educational performance and occupational horizons. Studies during the 1970s and 1980s, such as those by Clarricoates (1978) and Measor and Woods (1984), examined teacher perceptions and classroom processes and generally concluded that girls were cast into positions of passive docility. When girls did perform well at school, their success was likely to be explained by 'hard work and rule-following rather than brains or brilliance' (Walkerdine 1989: 268). Middle-class girls in particular have been perceived as 'doubly' docile – being attributed with neither the 'laddishness' of boys nor the 'brashness' of working-class girls (McRobbie 1978).

However, the conformity of middle-class girls may be more imagined than real. Arnot et al. (1999), in their analysis of the changing landscape of gender and education, claim that while the 'Victorian' representation of domesticated femininity was strongly present in post-war middle-class values, it had long been challenged by women of the upper middle class. For these women there was an alternative form of feminine success other than that of the 'intelligent wife' – that of the celibate career woman (Delamont 1989). This provided an important challenge to the male dominance of the academy and contributed to a female graduate elite. Indeed, the legacy of these upper middle-class pioneers was strongly felt and celebrated in some of the select-ive schools our female respondents attended. But, in addition, as our young women were growing up, they were also experiencing the changes asso-ciated with the increasing individualization and enterprise culture of the Thatcher years. Arnot *et al.* (1999) suggest that these changes enabled middle-class girls to develop academic ambitions that could be reconciled to a feminine rather than an androgynous (or lesbian) identity – albeit an identity that is dependent on the maintenance of clear class distinctions.

As girls have continued to outperform boys in public examinations, atten-tion has more recently focused upon school achievement and masculinity. In his classic study of working-class boys, Willis (1977) suggested that the celebration of the form of masculinity embedded within manual labour enabled the boys to draw on a cultural resource that compensated for, but also contributed to, their educational failure. Distinguished as 'lads', these boys labelled their peers with middle-class aspirations who worked hard at school as 'ear'oles'. That study was done at a time when there were still many manual occupations for unqualified 'lads'. But while demand for those forms of labour has sharply declined, 'doing well at school' is still often seen as a form of feminine behaviour (Harris 1995; Epstein 1998). Aggleton (1987) similarly draws on this association in his account of underachieving middle-class youth. His male students located themselves midway along a continuum of masculinity that ranged from the 'brutish manliness they associated with manual labour and the essential impotence they saw as characteristic of those whose involvement in mental labour was both com-mitted and industrious' (p. 73).

On the other hand, masculinity can be seen to be positively associated with academic achievement. Indeed, Connell (1989: 295) claims that what he terms 'hegemonic masculinity' is 'organised on the macro-scale around social power', defined in terms of access to higher education, entry to pro-fessions, command of communication and so on, and delivered to boys through their formal and informal identification as academic 'successes'. Although he also argues that boys who are deemed 'failures' can claim other sources of masculine power, such as physical aggression or sexual conquest, these are seen as marginal relative to the 'authorization of the hegemonic masculinity of the dominant group' (Connell 1996: 81). Within education, this form of masculinity can be epitomized by the traditional values of the elite public school in which boys are schooled into discipline, dress, academic hierarchy and team games (Heward 1988).

Studies such as these endorse the complexity of the relationship between class background and institutional context. They suggest a range of male and female sexualities at work, some of which seem to celebrate and reward academic achievement, with others seeming to stigmatize and hinder it. We explore how these tensions were evident in our respondents' accounts of how they endeavoured to negotiate a successful identity during their secondary school experiences.

Schoolboys and schoolwork

Much of the appeal of academically selective schools lies in the fact that they appear to offer environments that are protected from potentially 'unhelpful' peer group pressures. Although this is most extreme for students who board, the demands many selective schools make of students in terms of homework, sporting activities and, often, long travelling distances between home and school effectively serve to isolate pupils from 'outside' influences. As the then head of Nortown Grammar said when interviewed during the initial investigation of the Assisted Places Scheme, he could promise potential parents that the school would largely 'save' their sons from the worst excesses of adolescence – because academic demands would consume so much of their free time and because they would daily be in the company of academically able and academically ambitious pupils like themselves. It might be presumed that the privileged status many of our male respondents enjoyed at the start of their secondary schooling, in terms of socio-economic background and/or sponsorship or selection into these academic 'hothouses', would enable them to be incorporated within hegemonic masculinity as Connell describes it. However, their retrospective accounts suggest that this incorporation was far from straightforward and that the negative association between academic success and masculine identity which Willis and others highlighted is certainly not confined to working-class boys.

Within boys' schools that emphasize competition and hierarchy, the importance of academic success is clearly underscored. But some of these schools had also retained residues of the public school ethos of 'manliness' (Heward 1988), and perhaps some of its accompanying suspicion of undue cleverness. In these contexts, academic success alone might seem detrimental to the development of appropriately masculine identities:

> ... there were about four people in the class who ... worked hard, and they were the regular workers. And the ones who would always put their hands up, and so on, in lessons and everything. They were sort of, generally picked on, usually.
>
> (Edward Hawksley, Nortown Grammar)

Nor was there much sign in our interviews of new technologies being incorporated within legitimate forms of middle-class masculinity, as Connell (1996) has suggested.

> *SP*: Were there some people who didn't fit into Archbishop Ambrose?
> *Paul*: Yes, without a doubt.

SP: What were they like? Why didn't they fit in?
Paul: They were the academics.
SP: So you could be too academic?
Paul: Yes. They would call you something like 'geek'. You'd be into dungeons and dragons and computers. Things like that. You'd be totally unsporting and very academic minded.

In these contexts, academic success might seem detrimental to the development of appropriately masculine identities. One strategy to overcome this tension was to value academic success but to denigrate academic work. The importance of apparently effortless attainment has been documented by Aggleton (1987) and Mac and Ghaill (1994) in their studies of student subcultures. Despite the highly competitive nature of many of our male informants' schools, there was a strong incentive not to be seen to display academic ability too conspicuously or to appear too committed to academic work. As Brian (Bankside College) recalled: 'The thing to be seen to be was to never do any work and yet to do fairly well academically, but not too well so that you stand out'.

> People would appear to be better if they were seen to be doing less work. It wasn't there was a huge culture of no one doing any work and those that did were victimized. It was simply that the less you did, or were seen to do, the better you would look.
>
> (Hugh Bassey, Cathedral College)

As Edward Hawksley (Nortown Grammar) put it:

> You were supposed to make it look easy and never get caught working, and so nobody ever sat around the library all day, or anything like that. People would produce some work without any apparent effort, was the kind of ideal.

Boys who could not achieve without working sometimes developed ways of concealing their efforts to preserve their status in the peer group. Darren Leventhal (Archbishop Ambrose) suggested he had to work harder than other people, but recalled:

> When my friends sort of came round and they wanted to go out, I used to have to get my dad to go down and tell them that I was out, so I guess it was, yeah, I don't know, it was obviously just the friends that I've always had, to be keen was just a bad thing in school, I suppose.

The negative associations of being good at schoolwork were also reported by our ex-comprehensive boys. William Jowitt (Vicarage Road), for instance, remembered that being 'clever' meant 'you got a few jeers', while Christopher Scott (Rowton) recalled being called a 'swot' by people in his year at school. It is interesting to note that while our selectively-schooled boys were worried about being seen to work hard, our comprehensively-schooled boys were worried about being seen to work hard *and* about being thought of as 'too clever' by other pupils. They were therefore less inclined to cultivate an identity based on effortless achievement and more inclined to develop alternative strategies, such as sport or being 'cool' in other ways – as we discuss later. In as much as our comprehensively-schooled boys were less insulated from 'unhelpful' distractions, the academic risks of these alternative strategies were greater.

Schoolgirls and schoolwork

Although some of our young women also recall the stigma of being identified as a 'swot', they do not appear to have engaged in 'secret' work in the same way as their male counterparts. In general, and particularly at the selective schools, where there was greater academic pressure generally, the girls seemed to be less concerned at being seen to work hard. Indeed, for some girls, it was often unthinkable to deviate from the hard work ethic of the schools – even if one only did the 'minimum':

> I didn't work harder than anyone else. I always did my homework, but I didn't do anything else, I didn't do any extra. I don't know if that counts as not working hard, it probably doesn't, does it – doing everything you are supposed to do! I couldn't not do it. I couldn't bring myself not to work.
>
> (Harriet Barrett, Highgrove County)

The impression gained from accounts of these girls' schools was that there were few options other than striving for academic achievement, and that the route from O-levels or GCSEs to A-levels to university was automatically assumed to be the path most would follow: 'it was just one track and that was that' (Sacha Butcher, Dame Margaret's). Arnot *et al.* (1999: 111) suggest that 'upper- and upper-middle-class girls have been driven, even more than in the past, by the ambitions of their school to retain its place within the hierarchy of educational establishments'. Something of this is evident in Carol Joyce's account of Dame Margaret's:

> I just think some people couldn't cope under the pressure. Especially as it was an all girls' school. I think it can be a bit unhealthy at times . . . One of the girls had a nervous breakdown and had to go away for treatment. It was the kind of environment where they pressurized you; and if you were the type of person who pressurized yourself already, it probably didn't help to have more pressure put on you.

Girls at comprehensive schools, on the other hand, did recall being rather more anxious about being seen to work hard or to be unduly clever (Power *et al.* 1998a). And, like their male counterparts in comprehensive schools, devising ways of adapting in order to survive the peer pressure and gain social acceptance often meant not just hiding their efforts but hiding their ability. Sian Allan, a pupil at Moorside Comprehensive, had 'quite a rough time socially', on account of the peer pressure not to be successful, or 'not to admit to be successful':

> I mean there was peer group pressure not to be successful, or not to admit to be successful and I guess I learnt to pretend that I knew less than I did or to pretend that, whereas I had actually realized something half an hour ago, that I'd only just realized it . . . I was consciously aware of holding back so that other people could have a chance to think things through for themselves, so that I wasn't stepping in.

Valerie Nightingale, who went to Shirebrook, a comprehensive school which was reputed to have a strong academic tradition, referred to 'trying her hardest to do her worst' in order to gain acceptance among her friends: 'I felt that I didn't want to achieve, I didn't push myself to achieve because I would have stood out from the crowd I was involved in'. She too had deliberately not pushed herself to achieve for fear of standing out from the crowd in which she was involved: 'my peer group held me back, or I allowed them to hold me back . . . so I became a bit of a non-conformist and tried to go against the rules to fit in with everyone else.'

It is clear that for our young men and our young women, and irrespective of the kind of school attended, academic success was not commensurate with social success. If academic work was not to jeopardize social success, students had to develop alternative and achievable forms of identification.

Creating a more acceptable identity: boys

Several of our male respondents have indicated that it was important for them to achieve some kind of recognition within the school.

> There was this pressure to be top and good at things, and if you couldn't be that good, you didn't want to be mediocre. It was always . . . anything but mediocrity, you see.
>
> (Edward Hawksley, Nortown Grammar)

His school colleague, Craig French, identifies three routes through which you could 'define yourself out from the crowd':

> It was either being sporty, or being sort of sharp witted or a hard case basically . . . I remember in sort of things like assemblies, it was always about achievement and you certainly had to define yourself out from the crowd in one way or another whether that be being bright in later

years, being in the football or cricket team, or being a good fighter or whatever at a younger age.

Being sporty

Being 'good at games' provided boys with opportunities for recognition and could offset the undesirable attributes associated with academic work. Pete Emerson (Archbishop Ambrose) compared the teachers' 'interest in you being good academically' with the viewpoint 'of your peers [that] if you were very good at sport, then you were fairly cool and hard'. Michael Drossart (Bankside College) confirmed the significance of sport: 'in terms of someone staying at the school and enjoying life there, it was more important to be sporting than academic . . . the high flying academics were always teased, but the high flying sporties were never teased; you didn't dare.' Isaac Currie (Nortown Grammar) recalls how his ability at cricket helped him to overcome his isolation:

> I know I went through again a very bad time when I started at Nortown Grammar. I felt very isolated, very alone, didn't really make any friends. I remember taking a lot of stick from the other guys bearing in mind we were what about age 13, got a lot of stick from the other guys jibing me about my accent and coming all the way from the south and . . . I was very unhappy. But then after that it was quite ironic because as soon as the cricket season started, I made a lot more friends and got completely involved in that and from there on it was a fantastic time.

Brian Hogg (Bankside College) recalled a fellow pupil who was:

> brilliant and he worked like stink and he got As . . . he got As in every-thing, he never did not get an A and he went to Cambridge or Oxford or something, degree in a couple of years and got a star first, one of those, and at school, he was incredibly bookish, always had his nose in books, but he did his sports as well, got into the first team for football and played cricket as seconds and stuff, so he was OK because of that.

However, in schools where sporting prowess was given priority it could jeopardize rather than protect academic achievement. Geoff Pachul, a former pupil at Archbishop Ambrose, excelled in his academic work. He also participated actively in sports, playing rugby and cricket, and representing the county in athletics. Yet he recalled that he was not among the gang who thought they were 'cool', who tended to be in the rugby team, nor did he gain support from his school when he endeavoured to reduce his sporting activities in order to meet his academic demands:

> Although I played rugby, I was always on the fringes. I think there were a number of reasons. I didn't really like them and I didn't drink,

whereas everything they did in the evenings when they were on tour revolved around drinking. It wasn't that I didn't get on with them, but I didn't know how to be in their company and participate . . . They were all made prefects but I wasn't because I had withdrawn from the rugby team . . . Then I pulled out of the cricket team because they wanted me to play the day before my GCSEs. My dad was really angry because I was sent to the headmaster who convinced me to play. My dad went to the headmaster and told him that I wouldn't play. After that I was in their bad books.

For such schools, sport was very much a part of the exclusive school life, and seen as 'character building'. The commitment to sport, together with travelling time and homework, left pupils little time for social life outside school, perhaps, as we noted earlier, 'saving' them from those dangerous distractions of adolescence. By contrast, more of our male informants from comprehensive schools seemed to be involved in neighbourhood activities, including playing sport for local clubs, which represented a very different social world and one which could potentially lead them away from their schoolwork. Patrick Elamine, from Frampton, recalls how homework was done in the spaces left over between the football:

Where I live, it was opposite the park, and I was really into football. I mean, every night I may have had the best of intentions in the world to sit in my bedroom revising, but when I saw my friends outside, that was it!

Although soccer was linked to school in that he played for the school team, he also played for the district, in a local club and eventually, for a time, in the Northern League. As with many adolescent boys, sport, particularly football, took on great significance. Although, as we have seen, many academically selective schools also place value on sporting prowess, what is noticeable about Patrick is the extent to which his football was important for his outside-school identity rather than integral to his school identity – to the detriment of his academic achievement.

Being sharp-witted

Some of our male respondents, albeit a minority, countered the negative associations of 'being good' at school through cultivating 'wit'. Such subjectivities were not masculine in muscular terms but depended on a particular disposition to culture that celebrated cleverness without commitment and without visible effort.

It could, for instance, appear 'cool' to be clever or at least quick-witted. A more intellectual orientation to knowledge also made it possible to adopt identities that might be considered 'effeminate' in other contexts. Looking back to their time at Nortown Grammar, Colin identified languages, history and English as 'what the cool people did', and Edward Hawksley spoke of:

> A kind of a separate culture that they have, where . . . there were a certain number of kind of romantic figures who did English and they'd wear . . . They'd have kind of flicks and paisley shirts, and paisley ties.

As suggested above, even in those contexts, one had to be careful not to work so visibly that one's achievements were attributed to effort rather than to ability. As Bourdieu (1976) argues, the requirement that students develop the right kind of easy relationship with school advantages children from the higher social classes:

> What the child receives from an educated milieu is not only a *culture* (in objective sense), but also a certain style of relationship to the culture, which derives precisely from the *manner of acquiring it*. An individual's relationship with cultural works (and the mode of all his cultural experiences) is thus more or less easy, brilliant, natural, difficult, arduous, dramatic or tense according to the conditions in which he acquired his culture . . . It can be seen that by stressing the relationship with culture and setting great value on the most aristocratic style of relationship (ease, brilliance) school favours the most privileged children.
>
> (Bourdieu 1976: 117fn, original emphases)

The following comments provide a neat illustration of Bourdieu's view of cultural style and the easy 'distinction' so difficult for the less advantaged to display:

> SP: But you couldn't spot assisted place holders?
> Alex: No you couldn't spot them. But you could take an educated guess.
> SP: What would you look for in making that guess?
> Alex: As time progressed, it always tended to be the kid who always wore his jacket and tie and everything else, but didn't look quite right; he didn't wear it as it should have been worn, he wore it because the folks had bought it for him and he had to wear it.
> SP: How would somebody have worn it properly?
> Alex: Slightly more casual, slightly more natural, maybe slightly oversized as opposed to undersized. Or: 'this is part of me' rather than 'this is something I put on every morning to go to school'. It was the jacket with a bit of dirt and the odd fag burn in it, as opposed to the one that was brushed every morning before school.
>
> (Bankside College)

Boys from some backgrounds might have found it difficult to display a 'natural' ease in balancing school and peer-group expectations, but there were also dangers in appearing too refined.

> If you were academically able and also perhaps not . . . perhaps not particularly loud or particularly macho and from a fairly well-off background, then you were liable to be given stick for it; but if you could compensate for it socially, then you could sort of pass it off.
>
> (Colin, Nortown Grammar)

Certainly it appears that this kind of strategy was only possible within particular schools. None of our comprehensive schoolboys have described this kind of approach as a successful means of countering the negative associations of cleverness.

Being a 'hard case'

A third strategy involved the reinforcement of masculinity through the adoption of what might be called 'anti-school' dispositions and it was a strategy adopted by boys in all types of school. In its mildest form it might involve middle-class boys adopting some 'working-class' characteristics. Mac an Ghaill (1994) noted that his new middle-class male students developed a fantasy of 'proletarian authenticity', and it would appear that, in some contexts, middle-class students would attempt to 'pass' as working-class (a phenomenon also described by Aggleton 1987). Even within the exalted confines of Cathedral College, 'there were lots of people . . . who developed Cockney accents and things like that' (Alan, Cathedral College).

Similarly, Bryan Modest (Vicarage Road) recalled being given 'stick' by his friends when he did well, but his acceptance by the 'cool' crowd came about because he resolutely endeavoured *not* to be the 'boring boffin type':

> I was naughty . . . letting off the fire extinguisher, doing little pranks like that when you are a kid . . . that sort, like what not gets you accepted but it helped for me to have friends that are obviously wanting to do the same sort of things.

In addition to conventional rule-breaking involving smoking and drinking, some schoolboys described more serious misdemeanours, for example, Cliff Todd (Nortown Grammar):

> I mean I was as intelligent as anyone else there, it is just there . . . you know I started smoking when I was about 13 and sort of drinking and messing about with girls and then it moved on to drugs and you know . . . just generally a rebellious view . . . and the rebellious streak has just continued for a long time. Nothing particularly vicious, you know, I wasn't a bully as such . . . just things that you know I shouldn't really have done.

One respondent described this group as the lads who weren't 'stiff', who 'had a bit of mouth on them': 'we'd break a few rules because as far as we were concerned rules were there to be fractured and we'd see how far we could push rules, and we'd push our luck' (Duncan Mackay, Nortown Grammar). But when pushed to its limits, rebellion for some boys manifested itself in an outright rejection of academic values, culminating in drop-out from the school, with accompanying academic failure. Indeed, at its most extreme, it even resulted in expulsion from the school.

Creating a more acceptable identity: girls

The kind of strategies adopted by schoolboys were far less evident in our female respondents' accounts. While sport was seen as important by some of our female informants, it did not appear to carry the same status that it did for the boys, nor did it seem to be a substitute for academic success, particularly in the more academically pressured selective schools: 'I don't think they would have let you get away with it if you were just sporty and not academic' (Sacha Butcher, Dame Margaret's). A former pupil of St Hilda's, Cate Bozza, talked of sport and music being recognized, but the real rewards in school were for academic achievement, and friends who did not succeed academically tended to feel second rate, whatever their extra-curricular achievements. Very few of the girls mentioned sport when discussing what it took to succeed in their schools, and only one, a former comprehensive pupil, referred to gaining a higher profile with teachers in the classroom because of the relationship she had built up on the hockey field:

> I fitted in from about fourth year onwards because I got in with the sports crowd, played a lot of hockey and got some really good friends.
> (Annie Paisley, Milltown High)

The lack of emphasis on sport within girls' accounts may lead one to speculate that the negative association between academic career and female sexuality remains. Or it may reflect a negative association between physical ability and heterosexual femininity. As Rogers (1994) and Epstein and Johnson (1998: 115) claim, it is a common assumption that female PE teachers are 'by definition' lesbians.

Similarly absent in our girls' accounts are strategies connected with 'being hard'. There are accounts of 'rule-breaking' and 'rebelliousness', but the incidents are of a different order to those recounted by the boys. Resentment was expressed about some of the rules, which appeared 'petty', particularly in the girls' private schools, for example, 'going down the corridor the wrong way, wearing the wrong tights, the wrong schoolbag, even the wrong knickers', but more often the references from the girls at these schools related to *wanting* to rebel, rather than actually doing so:

I was too scared to . . . I wish I had, I mean the kind of things which were naughty are ridiculous and I wish I had done those kind of things . . . not wearing proper school uniform, completely shocking, and that's part of being an individual person and I don't think that is naughty or rebellious. It is just being individual, but I wouldn't have dared not to have my proper uniform on.

(Faith Kennedy, Dame Margaret's)

Indeed, far from wanting to cultivate a 'proletarian authenticity' in the manner of some of our male respondents, our middle-class girls sought to accentuate the distance between themselves and other female students. For middle-class girls in comprehensives, distance could be achieved through comparing themselves with working-class girls. Chloe Carter (Vicarage Road), for instance, talks about the 'other' girls:

They weren't really my kind of people, so they [would] . . . go off in the lunch times to have a smoke, they also got quite into shoplifting as well . . . we were quite high achievers and some of the others were bright. They were bright but they weren't really going for it . . . Jenny, I think she ended up, last time I saw her, she was in court for thieving. So it was a bit of a sliding scale . . . and there were a few girls that were real slaggish, they would be really covered in make-up.

In the more socially exclusive selective and private schools, the distinctions the girls fostered were more subtle – intra- rather than inter-class. The formation of distinctive cliques appears to be a frequent feature of middle-class girls' schools (see, for example, Delamont 1984) – cliques that were defined in terms of particular attributes and policed by what girls referred to as 'backbiting' and 'bitchiness'. The following accounts of social life at Dame Margaret's could apply to any of our elite private schools:

Girls that were square didn't wear the right clothes, weren't particularly attractive or were shy or unconfident . . . it was a very bitchy atmosphere at school. It was really quite horrible, and it was really survival of the fittest . . . if you weren't seen to be asserting your strength and leadership the whole time then you risked being picked on and even in the 'in-crowd' there would always be someone who was the one who might lose their place . . . so you had to constantly make sure you were doing the right thing.

(Claudia Wilton)

Cliques were tightly knit and depended on common (and exclusive) interests and dress codes – indicators of class distinction.

It was an image thing, the girls that were in this pretentious group, they were the ones that came from the wealthy background that had the horses and the tennis courts . . . The clever ones who were totally, a hundred per cent dedicated to their work to the point where nothing else featured in their lives, they all sort of hung around together. The ones who were obsessed with food, they all stuck together. The anorexics yeah, who literally could give you the calorie contents of anything you could possibly want to ask them. And then there was just like ordinary people, normal ones.

(Celia Fyfe)

These cliques may well represent differences between students from the old and the new middle class. There are strong parallels here with the cliques identified by Delamont (1984) in her ethnography of St Luke's, a private girls' school in Scotland. Celia's reference to those 'that had the horses and the tennis courts' were often from the old middle-class backgrounds of Delamont's 'debs' and 'dollies'. Those 'clever ones' were more likely to be from new middle-class backgrounds, although many of our students from these backgrounds displayed far more 'stylish' and 'cool' behaviour than Delamont's 'swots' and 'weeds'. Across all of our female respondents, accounts of relationships with boys are relatively absent in their retrospective accounts, but where they do appear, they also indicate an awareness of the 'right' kind of boy. As Carol Joyce, recalls: 'Going out with boys from Clifton Grammar was considered "super cool"'.

These accounts appear to endorse Arnot *et al.*'s (1999: 111) conclusion that the gains of girls' individualism, and particularly that of middle-class girls, are based upon a subversion of the patriarchal order, but are also 'associated with a series of damning comparisons with other girls'. Middle-class girls do appear to have succeeded in developing a feminized academic identity, but one that is heavily inscribed by social class.

Coeducation versus single-sex schooling

As we noted above, the then headteacher of Nortown Grammar claimed that his school 'protected' his boys from the distractions of adolescence. Claims such as these are even more commonly made about girls' schools. In this final section, we briefly examine these claims through our respondents' perceptions of single-sex schooling in general, and of the value of girls' schools in particular.

The gender-related differences in academic achievement that our data identified in many cases related to school type, which, as we have pointed out, in our sample tended to correspond with single-sex and coeducational status. In the survey, we had asked respondents whether they felt girls did better when educated separately from boys. Twice as many of the respondents from coeducational schools (51 per cent) disagreed with this statement

Table 6.1 Respondents' perceptions on single-sex education for girls by sex and school type

	Sex of respondent		
	Male	Female	Total
Pupils from single sex schools			
Agree	31	59	90
	(26%)	(60%)	(42%)
Neutral	51	19	70
	(43%)	(19%)	(32%)
Disagree	36	20	56
	(31%)	(20%)	(26%)
Total	118	98	216
	(100%)	(100%)	(100%)
Pupils from coeducational schools			
Agree	9	16	25
	(18%)	(20%)	(19%)
Neutral	14	24	38
	(28%)	(30%)	(30%)
Disagree	27	39	66
	(54%)	(49%)	(51%)
Total	50	79	129
	(100%)	(100%)	(100%)

compared with the former pupils of single-sex schools (26 per cent). But when views were broken down according to gender, we found it was the girls from single-sex schools who were much more likely to support the positive advantages of being educated separately (60 per cent). Boys who had been to single-sex schools were more likely to feel neutral about this issue, or to disagree (Table 6.1).

Endorsing the survey data, our female informants in the interviews were, on the whole, more ready to comment about the impact of segregation or combined education. In supporting the academic merits of single-sex education, their comments echoed other findings in the research literature (Mahony 1985; Leonard 1996; Smithers and Robinson 1997). Many talked of girls' self-consciousness in front of boys, particularly during puberty, when sexual differences become more apparent, and 'your hormones kick in'. Sadie Manners at Milltown recalled 'the pressure ... when you are 15 or 16, you don't want to make yourself look stupid, but especially not in front of a boy! That makes it even worse!' Similarly, Carol Joyce at Dame Margaret's considered the presence of boys in the classroom would have been detrimental to her:

I was quite shy and I think boys are naturally louder. Whereas I felt quite encouraged in the classroom at Dame Margaret's High School, I could easily have been one of those people who sat at the back of the class and didn't say anything, and who didn't develop and do well.

Many had gone to coeducational primary schools, and recalled their early experiences: 'the boys would kick you in the shins and pinch you and were more demanding in the classroom. And the girls would sit down and shut up and get on with work' (Tamsin Nee, St Hilda's).

We have shown earlier that the gender gap in terms of subject choice was narrower in single-sex schools, perhaps a reflection of the educational feminism that was celebrated in them. Karina Park talked of her headmistress at Parkside, our only single-sex comprehensive, being on a 'mission to prove that women could do science', though she herself studied languages. Milltown High similarly instilled a strong feminist awareness in its pupils, according to Annie Paisley:

> socially it was that everybody had to get on and that we were all sisters . . . they did pressure us towards science, towards the male subject, they kept on, 'we are as good as boys, we are good as men, we could do anything.' Which is a shame really because a lot of us did prefer the arts.

But there was some evidence of this in coeducational comprehensive schools. Sian Allen felt that Moorside had shielded her from the sexism she encountered later in her career:

> Girls were encouraged to do physics and that sort of thing and not to do traditionally girlie subjects and we were encouraged to apply for universities, you know, the best that we were likely to be accepted by and all the rest of it really. We were encouraged, not held back . . . that was in large measure . . . I remember that the head of sixth form was very keen on the girls having opportunity and that was great and it is only since then that I have become aware of what discrimination is and how it works.

At sixth form, a few of our informants experienced moves either into or out of single-sex and coeducational schools. For Mark Saheed (Vicarage Road), going from a mixed comprehensive school to a boys' private school for the sixth form, the change hardly deserved comment: 'it wasn't as if you just went from a mixed class and then just hung about with boys 24 hours of the day for the next two years. And we were getting to the age when we were starting to mix with girls anyway so it didn't really make that much difference.' Olga Bundy, on the other hand, moved from Highgrove County to Milltown Grammar for the sixth form, where she was one of only 18 girls in a school of 300 boys. She found this much more of a challenge. Although ready to admit she might have done better academically elsewhere, she found the experience invaluable socially. She highlighted the contrasts that she had experienced in the two schools. At Highgrove 'we were expected to behave well and to be intelligent and to be articulate and to put our hands up and to be good at science and to be good at maths.' Her decision to go to Milltown Grammar she admitted was primarily because it was a boys' school. There she found that as a girl 'I was seen as fragile and I wasn't expected to be fiercely intelligent and I was treated very differently, and . . . there is a tendency for the teachers to expect boys to answer the questions and not the girls.' However, Olga had no regrets. In her view, Highgrove County, free from the presence of boys, had allowed its pupils to concentrate on education, building their self-confidence to go through the early teenage years without being teased or worried. She considered this early experience had been a really good foundation for life, including her time at Milltown Grammar.

The idea of girls and boys coming together in the sixth form was, however, one that received some support in our interviews, largely because of the social advantages. Many of our informants drew attention to the artificial nature of single-sex schooling, which shielded pupils from the competitive demands of a mixed gender society outside. Leaving this protected world could generate a culture shock: 'it would have been useful to mix with other guys, and have to fight for your opinion and have to push your point of view forward a bit more strongly, because that is what you have to do in real life, that's what you have to do in business' (Natalie Jackman, Highgrove County). Harriet Barrett, who had also been to Highgrove County, found she was still disadvantaged by her single-sex schooling within higher education. Once again, it came down to a question of self-confidence. In seminars, she described finding it hard to speak and ask questions:

> I have to steel myself, and often the moment passes because I'm trying to work out how to say it. And a lot of men seem to have the confidence that I don't have . . . all that time I was growing up I never worked out how I could put myself across in mixed company.

Epstein (1996) has noted that the requirement that boys actively promote a visibly and unambiguously masculine identity appears to decrease significantly at the sixth form stage, when working hard academically may not carry a social risk and may even be expected. Redman and Mac an Ghaill (1997) link this change with the move from compulsory state education to the labour market or further and higher education, that requires new forms of identity or what they term 'muscular intellectualness'.

In our sample, as career aspirations generally in the sixth form began to take on more substance and significance, the negotiated gender identities of both girls and boys appeared more secure. For some boys, hard work became a more acceptable masculine attribute perhaps because it became more closely connected to entry to male professional status. Cliff Todd, a former pupil of Nortown Grammar, had early on prided himself on his apparent left-wing stance: 'pretending to be like Derek Hatton when basically I was kind of from a stable middle-class home in Highgrove'. Intending to appear rougher than he actually was, he had rebelled against the conformity of his school by fraternizing with the 'lads' who wore bubble coats and trainers, who had smoked, drunk, dated girls and broken the rules. He recalled the way his attitude changed in the sixth form:

> You realize that you are not going to get anywhere in life if you think big and tough and macho. You know you can do all those things but just keep it quiet and get on with it . . . I felt a lot more respect towards the teachers . . . they treated you more like adults . . . I just wanted to get A-levels, and also I was able to concentrate on the subjects I enjoyed . . . so my academic and my sort of social personality changed dramatically in the sixth form. I mean I suppose it was sort of a case of growing up one level.

Girls, too, who had struggled to fit in during their early years at secondary school, talked of increased confidence by the time they got to sixth form:

> I became more self-assured in my own identity . . . I suppose I just, yeah, I just felt I was maturing and I felt I suppose quite secure of my position in school and my friends and whatever.
>
> (Lara Felton, Milltown High)

In this chapter, we have briefly looked at some of the ways in which our middle-class girls and boys sought to reconcile the academic expectations of their homes and their schools with peer group cultures that made school-work, or at least the visible engagement with schoolwork, problematic. There appear to be both similarities and differences in the strategies developed by boys and girls. Elsewhere (Power *et al.* 1998a) we have speculated on how the gendered nature of involvement may contribute to boys' relative underachievement. Some of the strategies developed by middle-class girls may be less damaging to their academic performance. However, even among our female respondents, the 'cliquey' cultures could contribute to anxieties and insecurities. For many of our boys and girls these anxieties were over-come as they progressed through sixth form and into universities. For others, though, their experiences left legacies that could interrupt or impair these transitions. We examine the upward progression of our respondents in the next chapter.

7 Middle-class students and university: 'fish in water'?

Bourdieu (1990: 108) claims that middle-class children 'move in their world as fish in water', an analogy borrowed by Ball *et al.* (2002) in their analysis of young people's university choices. While higher education is undoubtedly alien territory to many children from working-class backgrounds, we question again the implied homogeneity of middle classness and the consequently assumed ease of progression. In this chapter, we continue to explore how differences between middle-class families make the progression more or less easy and how higher education careers are often complicated or uncertain even for those who might be expected to glide through university like 'fish in water'.

School achievement and university destination

As reported in Chapter 4, the great majority of our students obtained the number of A-levels considered necessary for the next stage of their progression to middle-class adulthood. Despite their overall success, however, there were significant differences in A-level performance as measured by the standard university admissions criterion of A-level point scores. These differences appeared at school level, and reflect variation within as well as between sectors (Table 4.3). And even slight differences could produce significantly different opportunities for both male and female pupils to translate school achievements into high-status university places. In general, as we show now, those from private schools had been significantly more successful at getting into the more prestigious universities. Before exploring this finding in some detail, we need to set it in context.

As long as university entry was highly restricted, as it was in the 1930s when the age participation rate was 7 per cent, graduate qualifications were irrelevant for most middle-class occupations. Even among the latest cohort included in the Oxford Mobility Study, about two-thirds of the men in Service Class occupations had gone to a selective secondary school but only 5 per cent of the managers and only 20 per cent even of the professionals had university degrees (Goldthorpe 1982: 174). But the university population grew fourfold between the late 1940s and the late 1980s, the time when our informants were considering joining it and when the age-participation rate first crossed the 15 per cent 'border' commonly taken to mark the shift from an 'elite' to a 'mass' system. As universities came to be viewed as the main locations of 'top ability', 'mere' possession of a degree lost some of the occupational advantages previously attached to it and intensified competition for the more prestigious locations. This has focused a great deal of research attention on socially stratified access to a socially stratified system – that is, on the extent to which students in the most prestigious institutions and following the more prestigious courses of study are unrepresentative of the population at large (Heath and Clifford 1996). In France, for example, expansion reduced social class differences in overall participation in higher education but left them untouched in entry to the Grandes Écoles. In the most prestigious of those institutions in the mid-1990s, children of the *cadres moyens et supérieurs* made up 90 per cent of the student body compared with 60 per cent in the 'mass' universities and only 30 per cent on low-status vocational courses (Duru-Bellat 2000; Galland and Oberti 2000).

As Bourdieu had noted earlier, expanded educational provision might lead non-traditional recruits to expect what it had given others when people like them were still excluded. And the wider availability of previously rationed credentials is likely to bring defensive responses from the previously advantaged that are likely to include the 'multiplication of subtly ranked paths', which create new branching points where 'access to the dominant class is decided' (Bourdieu 1984: 154–5). In the absence of objective ways of comparing graduate qualifications, either as measures of specialized knowledge or (except by inference from the kinds of students likely to have been recruited) as proxy measures of general ability and personal qualities, the interests of Bourdieu's 'dominant groups' are best served by choosing and being chosen by the 'best' university (Morley 1997). Knowing which qualifications to seek and where to acquire them in a complex and stratified market are dimensions of cultural competence most readily available to applicants not only from 'educated' homes but also from schools with the know-how to read the system and its more specific requirements (Bourdieu 1998). It involves not only identifying 'the best' but having the confidence to regard it as within reach. All this has directed public as well as research attention to socially stratified university entry, and to the well documented fact that social and educational exclusiveness 'declines with the status of the university' (Adonis and Pollard 1998: 24). In 1998–99, for example, average points scores at 15 widely if unofficially accepted 'top' universities were over 25; at eight of the 'new' universities they were below 12 (*Financial Times* 8–9 April 2000). In that year, over 70 per cent of entrants to Cambridge, Oxford, Bristol, Nottingham, Edinburgh, the London School of Economics and University College London were from social classes I and II, compared with a third or below at (for example) the universities of East and North London, Paisley, Wolverhampton and Thames Valley. The close alignment of high entry scores with high proportions of middle-class and privately schooled students might be taken as an unavoidable consequence of entry on academic merit. But a report from the Sutton Trust (2000) estimated that the proportion of entrants to the five 'best' universities was significantly higher than the benchmark 'target', which takes A-level performance into account, and that even very able children from poor families and from comprehensive schools were substantially under-represented. Its conclusion was that 'the field from which the country recruits its future elite is extraordinarily narrow'.

Although the comparative ranking of universities other than Oxford and Cambridge received less public attention in the late 1980s when our informants were making their choices, which was just before the sharp status boundary between universities and polytechnics was ostensibly removed, there was a close relationship between their A-level points and the status of the university they attended. Of course, university status is contested, and different universities have different reputations for specific areas of expertise. Nevertheless, as with schools, it is possible to rank universities along a rough hierarchy of prestige,[1] with Oxbridge and other élite old universities at the top and new universities and colleges of higher education at the bottom. If the A-level points obtained by our respondents are tabulated against the rank of their university destination, there is a clear and obvious relationship. Nearly two-thirds of those who went to Oxbridge had 30 or more A-level points (equivalent to at least three A grades at A-level) and over two-thirds of those who went to new universities had 14 points or fewer (equivalent to fewer than two Cs and an E) (see Table 7.1).

The close relationship between A-level performance and university destination might prompt the conclusion that the transition from school to higher education is based on a rational matching of ability to course. However, respondents' accounts of their aspirations, and of how they managed the process of securing a place, reveal significant leeway for manoeuvre at the boundaries of what are 'acceptable' grades and illustrate the importance of

Table 7.1 Relationship between A-level points (without General Studies) and university destination

Type of university	A-level points							
	0–4	5–9	10–14	15–19	20–24s	25–29	30+	Total
Oxbridge				1	3	12	30	46
				(2%)	(7%)	(26%)	(65%)	(100%)
Other elite	1		1	2	13	13	16	46
	(2%)		(2%)	(4%)	(28%)	(2%)	(35%)	(100%)
Other 'old'	4	2	15	19	50	30	11	131
	(3%)	(2%)	(11%)	(15%)	(38%)	(23%)	(8%)	(100%)
'New'/CHEs	9	11	23	13	7			63
	(14%)	(18%)	(36%)	(21%)	(11%)			(100%)
Total	14	13	39	35	73	55	57	286
	(5%)	(5%)	(14%)	(12%)	(26%)	(19%)	(20%)	(100%)

the social and institutional processes at work in 'matching' student to university.

The social dimensions of choice

In their investigation of inter-relationships between class, culture and high-status university destinations, Brown and Scase (1994: 58) describe the progress of middle-class children 'through a succession of nannies, preparatory and boarding schools to an extended childhood at sheltered colleges and finishing schools, [so that] achievement in this system appears natural, if not always effortless'. This stereotypical description bears little resemblance to the educational backgrounds of our sample of students. It is nevertheless the case that, for some students, progressing to higher education was seen as an inevitable stage in their transition to adulthood. Lana Giblin, for example, claimed that:

> I never thought that I wouldn't go to university . . . all the way along, it never entered my head that I wouldn't go to university . . . I don't think we really thought about it at Dame Margaret's, most people assumed they would go on . . . I don't know if we ever really discussed it.

For some students at elite private schools, there were tacit expectations not just about going to university but about going to the right kind of university. Some of our respondents not only had clear university aspirations in their early teens, they also knew even then which Oxbridge college they intended to apply for. Brown and Scase claimed that this familiarity and 'naturalness'

Table 7.2 University destination by type of assets held by father
(Class III NM and above)

Status of university destination	Father's middle-class assets type			
	Cultural	Organizational	Entrepreneurial	Total
1. Elite	52	20	3	75
% of type	37	31	50	36
2. Other 'old'	64	28	1	93
% of type	46	43	17	44
3. 'New' and CHEs	24	17	2	43
% of type	17	26	33	20
Total	140	65	6	211
% of total	66	31	3	100

of progression was evident in students from both professional and managerial backgrounds. Our data do not support this, perhaps reflecting Perkin's (1989) assertion that Oxbridge is 'the main articulator of the social ideal of the professional class'. Clearer university aspirations, and a relatively higher access to elite universities, might be expected where parents' own socio-economic status derives more from cultural than from organizational assets (Table 7.2). We return to this point later in the chapter.

High levels of achievement at school and entry into high-status universities and high-status courses were certainly more common among our privately educated respondents, who also tended to come from higher-level socio-economic backgrounds. Although detailed analysis of the extent to which schools are simply reproducing rather than interrupting processes of social and cultural inheritance would have been impossible in a sample of this size, the widely reported relationship between the level of parental education and student attainment was evident even within a cohort of academically able students. Those whose parents had higher education were more likely to attend university than those whose parents had no higher education. In the private sector, 95 per cent of students from homes where the mother had higher education also went on to university. In the state sector as a whole, the figure was 89 per cent and for comprehensives it was just over 90 per cent. These figures lend some support to those middle-class professional parents who feel relatively 'safe' in sending their children to at least the more academically oriented comprehensive schools.

Our middle-class students from backgrounds with less cultural capital of this kind had less clear aspirations. This was particularly true of those from comprehensive schools, who had often remained unsure until late in their school careers whether or not they would go on to higher education. They sometimes seemed to have 'arrived' at decisions about their higher education only at the very last minute. Jamie Cornwall and Bernadette Glassford, whose fathers were a farmer and a production supervisor, recalled:

> There's been no long plan – everything has been done at the last minute . . . What I were going to do after the end of my A-level course, I were either going to finish, or go to . . . college and I were either going to do an HND, or a degree. I didn't want to leave home, because it's so easy to work, but it's more pressure off my Dad rather than me that I go. And then it unfolded; I got an A in my geology A-level. So I thought well I'll go and do a geology degree. Because I thought I were pretty good at it by that time . . . I never went to any careers advisor. Actually, when I got my results, it was in August, 26th of August it was, I run to my geology teacher and said 'Can I get on a course anywhere?' And he said, 'Well, I don't think you'll get on one now, you know, this year.' So I applied to Derby then, and I nearly gone on it, well I could have gone, but I didn't take it because it was too far. Away from home, you see. And so what I did, I turned that down and I re-took my geography to improve it from a grade D, but it weren't a grade D, they'd made a mistake, it were a grade C . . . what they had actually done, in the topic I had to do, my project, they forgot to add that to my score. I think it was about October that I was resitting this, after about a month or two, this letter come through, and Manchester university, which I'd applied to, said they wanted a grade C in geography, but I'd got it then, so I didn't need to do that!
>
> (Jamie Cornwall, Moorside)

> I don't even remember how I chose my university. I think I just picked up a few brochures and I remember it was a Sunday night and the application had to be in for Monday morning. I was just on my way out and I just picked them up and just 'Oh, yeah I'll go here' . . . I went to Newcastle. I went to the polytechnic – it was a polytechnic. I applied to Leeds and Sheffield universities, Newcastle Polytechnic. With the grades I got I could have got into Leeds. I don't know what made me choose but I just thought I am going to go to Newcastle.
>
> (Bernadette Glassford, Parkside)

Their lack of clear strategy and, in Bernadette's case, the selection of a lower-status university destination than her A-level grades would have made available reflect a lack of familiarity with higher education in general, and perhaps that lack of confidence about going for ambitious options to which we will return. For students such as Lizzie Hayward (Cherry Tree), there appears to have been little guidance at home or school:

> When I chose my university, it was all a bit of a haze to me really. There was no support from the school at all really in that area. I think I spent just one evening and ticked the boxes, with no in-depth thought

about what I was doing. So I think I was fortunate really because the course at Sheffield Hallam was very very good. And it's a highly thought of course. And I could have ended up with something I didn't enjoy at all . . . I don't think I got any advice – I certainly have no feeling of any advice. We were just given the handbook really. And I never thought of doing anything which wasn't one of the A-levels I was doing. I never thought about a wider selection, or something more job related, or whatever. It was just, what A-level do you do best? And that was your degree. And I enjoyed the history degree, so I don't think I would have changed that, but I'd have liked to know there were other opportunities there really.

Our findings support the conclusion of Ball *et al.* (2002) that the 'accuracy' of prestige rankings (that is, where students' rankings most closely coincided with a commonly used university league table) was highest among those choosers who came from a family where members had previously 'used' higher education or from schools with strong track records in higher education progression. Those from managerial and intermediate backgrounds also seemed to pay more attention to attending 'local' universities to stay close to either family or friends, as is evident in Jamie Cornwall's account above and also that of Nadia Healey (Cherry Tree), who wanted to go to Sheffield but ended up at Westminster University:

> I didn't really have any career in mind at that time . . . Estate management seemed to be a nice balance between being out and about and being stuck in the office. So I looked into that and it sounded perfect. I would be a surveyor, that's what I was going to be . . . there weren't too many places doing it. I wanted to go to Sheffield desperately just because some friends were going there and I'd always wanted to go since I was young and it was close to home but they didn't do the course so I couldn't do that. And then they introduced the course the next year, I was very unhappy. I ended up in London and then left.

Even when their A-level grades would have enabled them to consider Oxbridge as a realizable destination, these students felt it was 'not for them' or were worried about trying and failing. Both kinds of 'refusal' were more common among those with parents in lower-status middle-class occupations, such as Isaac Cordell and Neil Gresham, who were both from Frampton and whose fathers were respectively a further education lecturer and a Merchant Navy officer:

> I didn't want to go to Oxford or Cambridge. Durham was my first choice. I didn't apply to Oxford or Cambridge because I didn't want to go through the palaver of applying when I knew I wouldn't fit in.
>
> (Isaac Cordell)

The sort of people who did go on for it were, I don't know actually, they were able. They were the cleverest ones but I think they reached a high standard but they did tend to be slightly better brought up. That sounds ridiculous. I guess actually, I don't want to sway it too much that way but probably if I am honest, there probably was a bit of fear in there as well. Fear of failure. I didn't want to go for it and fail.

(Neil Gresham)

Students whose parents had been to higher education were less likely to have felt anxious about failing. These students were often found within the significant minority (15 per cent of the sample) who had expressed an ambition to go to Oxbridge at the start of their secondary school careers. Most of these were at private schools. Forty-six (13 per cent) succeeded, although, as we show in the next chapter, these were not all among those for whom Oxbridge had been an early aspiration. They were, however, likely to regard it as an achievable ambition, even in some cases as a family tradition, rather than as a distant and strange place:

My oldest brother went to Oxford ... He again had been through the Cathedral College conveyor belt if you like. He was a brilliant mathematician, walked into Oxford ... My other brother ... was at Cambridge, so there was a real sort of Oxbridge history to it but again it wasn't something that was pressured in that way. It was obviously there ... my parents could have been very pushy about this sort of thing but I just don't think they were. I don't remember them being pushy – but if they were it was far too subtle for me to realize.

(Anthony Jolly, Cathedral College)

Our findings resemble those of Ball *et al.* (2002), who found among their sample of 'choosers' that the 'first choice' of university was class-related, with 78 per cent of Oxbridge 'choosers' coming from 'upper' middle-class backgrounds compared with only 27 per cent from this class electing to go to the new universities. For some of our informants, choice of university was heavily directed, even constrained.

You kind of get into the treadmill and you never think of anything else because that's what, you know, it's the classic, this is what is expected, you go along and you do it. I kind of wanted a year out, but was too scared and I didn't know what do in it and all the rest of it. So I thought 'Oh well, university, you know, what else am I going to do?' They suggested 'Do you want to go to Oxford or Cambridge?', and I was like, 'What, is that the only choice?'

(Celia Fyfe, Dame Margaret's)

Parental expectations of and familiarity with higher education usually advantaged our respondents, but several had reacted against such prompting.

The following recollection is also interesting because of Cate Bozza's (St Hilda's) claim that Cambridge was the 'only one' that did architecture, which suggests that other universities were out of the frame of reference, and her perception that going to Bath University was an act of rebellion. A similar stance is reflected in the later comment by Hugh Durack (Nortown Grammar) about his very mildly rebellious choice of King's College London.

> Well once I'd thought about architecture, Cambridge is the only one that does it and I went to an open day and I didn't like the atmosphere . . . I'd have to say I was in a rebellious frame of mind and thought I'm not bloody going there because everybody else was going and there was a whole thing of they read out the names of people who went to Oxbridge in assembly and nobody else got read out when they got into university and it just annoyed the hell out of me. So for better or worse I rebelled.
>
> (Cate Bozza)

> I'm still not entirely sure why I didn't go for Oxbridge. I think part of it was a rebellion in that I just didn't want to follow the line of going to Oxbridge like everybody else did.
>
> (Hugh Durack)

As we explore in the next chapter, not all aspirations were realized. Some of our respondents did not get good enough grades, or failed the Oxbridge entrance tests or interview. In the few cases where they had not accepted their situation and chose to challenge it, it is clear that the individuals had sufficiently high levels of cultural and social confidence to be able to overcome the setback:

> I was quite happy that I got four passes. It got me where I wanted to go. I didn't have enough for the university I wanted, but I phoned them up . . . I'd gone the previous Easter for a few days to meet them all so I just phoned them up and said 'Let me on'. And because he knew me, because he had met me, he said 'Yeah', which was very galling for people I met at university who didn't get on my course that had really wanted to – because it was a prestigious course.
>
> (Annie Paisley, Milltown High)

> I was more disappointed when at one stage I thought I hadn't got into St Andrews. I had to phone up for a week to haggle.
>
> (Selina Webster, Highgrove County)

> Well I mean basically I missed my offer to Edinburgh by a point and I remember when I got my results that day, being absolutely devastated because my heart was set on Edinburgh . . . and so I just spent I think the rest of the day ringing Edinburgh and writing and I mean I got in on the fact, through my hard work.
>
> (Karen Nixon, Dame Margaret's)

Table 7.3 Rank of higher education destinations (%) by school sector

	Private (n = 160)	*State (n = 137)*
1. Elite	43.1	16.8
2. Other 'old'	44.4	43.8
3. New and CHEs	12.5	39.4

The influence of school

There is little doubt that better overall performance of our privately educated respondents at A-level enabled them to secure a higher proportion of places at the more prestigious universities. Nearly one-half (43 per cent) of those from private schools went to 'top rank' universities and only one in eight went to the lowest rank. Conversely, of those who went to state schools, including the grammar schools, only one in six went to elite destinations, and two out of five went to rank 3 universities (Table 7.3).

The 'success' of the private sector does not necessarily, and certainly not simply, reflect a greater capacity to 'bring out the best' in academically able pupils. It also reflects a concerted drive to channel students into high-status universities by encouraging high aspirations and discouraging less 'ambitious' choices, having special provision for potential Oxbridge entrants and sometimes having detailed knowledge of and actual contacts with particular colleges. These resources are especially useful to students from backgrounds with relatively little in the way of educational inheritance. We have noted that the children of parents who had been to university were likely to progress to university largely irrespective of the kind of school attended. However, there does appear to be a significant sector difference in the extent to which students were likely to progress to higher education if their parents were not graduates. Low levels of educational inheritance appear to have made only insignificant difference to the A-level performance of those who attended private schools and grammar schools provided that they stayed long enough to benefit.

Aiming high

Just as it was expected that many of our middle-class students would progress to higher education, it was also expected that their destinations would be at least the 'respectable' universities. The binary line had not yet been formally dissolved, and polytechnics were not considered acceptable alternatives for students at private and grammar schools. As Rachel Apple and Naomi Sharples (Highgrove County) recalled:

I remember flicking through the big handbook about courses, and they were mainly academic subjects. I think as well there was a big divide when I was in the sixth form between the polytechnics and the universities, and it wasn't really considered that you'd go to polytechnic.

(Rachel Apple)

Everyone applied to university. There wasn't much thought of polytechnics although they were obviously mentioned. We had careers lessons, they said 'Well you could apply to polytechnics too'. But that wasn't pushed and it was very much 'Well apply for universities but, if you want to, apply for polytechnics because then you'll have something to fall back on.'

(Naomi Sharples)

Lara Felton (Milltown High) had been actively discouraged from applying to a polytechnic and only felt able to do so after she had left the school:

I actually think I began to think what I wanted to do after I'd left school, because I took a year out after sixth form and I think it was that time that I saw lots of opportunities that didn't really exist within. I mean I got really frowned on at school for wanting to apply through PCAS [Polytechnics Central Admissions System] for at that time the polytechnics wasn't really seen as appropriate for girls leaving Milltown and they're very keen on just pushing for university applications strictly, and it's very kind of Oxford/Cambridge.

When she recalls her academic career now, Lara wishes she had felt 'proud that I was going on to higher education, rather than feeling I was thick for going to a poly rather than a university.'

At the 'top' end of the hierarchy, getting high numbers of students into Oxbridge is a large part of the appeal of the kinds of private school our informants attended, as well, no doubt, as a matter of belief in the consequent advantages and of the university experience of many of the teaching staff. The highlighting of Oxbridge entrance rates creates the view, if only by implication, that those are the only truly desirable destinations.

Everybody did it really, and so there was quite a lot of pride at stake. I mean everybody had to sort of go for it, at least give it a go. I mean in my year 40 people got into Oxford and Cambridge. And then the year before it had been something similar, it's that sort of ratio they get.

(Elizabeth Murdoch, St Hilda's)

> The school did take the Oxbridge candidates pretty seriously . . . they definitely thought they were more important and they gave them the extra tuition for the Oxford Entry Exam.
>
> (Hugh Bassey, Cathedral College)

Lana Giblin, who left Dame Margaret's for Cathedral College at the sixth-form stage, recalled how 'half the year applied to Oxbridge . . . and if you didn't get in the first year then you took a year off and tried again.' This kind of pressure meant that anything below Oxbridge was likely to seem 'second best'.

> We were quite indoctrinated that basically everyone had to try to go to Oxbridge, and if you didn't get in you went somewhere else. That was . . . the kind of indoctrination we received.
>
> (Louise Boot, St Hilda's)

> I think in my year, my sixth form year . . . two-thirds of us had Oxbridge offers. I think at that point it was the best year they'd ever had . . . We came top of the table, that sort of thing . . . It was obscene. That is the right word to describe it as, because of course what it meant was those people that didn't were 'Oh my God, I only got into Bristol.' That's just so skewed. In fact, one of my best mates now, who I was at [school] with . . . he went to Bristol and he's a very intelligent kid, didn't get into Peterhouse Cambridge to do economics, and I know he still feels bitter about that because in some way ever since school he's seen himself as, that's failing, and it's not at all.
>
> (Anthony Jolly, Cathedral College)

All this may be 'rational' in the calculative sense to which we referred earlier, as the 'archetypical elite route', which has been 'part of the reality and folklore of British educational and social life' (Reid *et al.* 1991: 17), has been a narrow one running into Oxford or Cambridge through a very few public schools. Privileged links between elite private schooling and higher education have been concentrated on those two universities to a much greater extent than, for example, in the United States (Cookson and Persell 1985). As the number of university places multiplied, the private sector's share of the total entry inevitably fell sharply from 25 to 19 per cent between 1987 and 1992. But its representation among entrants to Oxford rose over that same period from 37 to 48 per cent (Heward and Taylor 1993). In their anatomy of the new super-class, Adonis and Pollard (1998) located its predominant higher education firmly in Oxford and Cambridge. Given our informants' experience of universities such as Bristol being considered 'second best', it is hardly surprising that universities lower down the status hierarchy were rarely considered. Carol Joyce (Dame Margaret's) remembered her own dilemma on failing to get the grades she needed for a place at Exeter University:

It never occurred to me. All my friends had got the grades they needed for university: Julie went to Cambridge, Anna went to York, Mandy had decided to take a year out but had a deferred place at Nottingham, Sophie went to Bristol. So all my friends were going to what I perceived to be good universities; so there was no way I was going to go to a poly. I would rather not have gone; that's how strongly I felt about it.

There is little evidence of any comparable pressure from our ex-comprehensive school pupils, although some highlighting of Oxbridge entrants was remembered from speech days. On the other hand, some of our comprehensive school interviews gave clear indications of the effects of self-selection, of able students regarding an Oxbridge place as unattainable, or inappropriate, or likely to prove 'uncomfortable' for someone like them. Amelia Otis (Vicarage Road), for example, had

> thought about it, and my parents wanted me to, and I did go and look around. But I never really got the encouragement when I was doing A-levels . . . And I never felt that anybody was very sure that I was going to have any chance and therefore I didn't feel myself that I had any chance and I didn't apply.

This was a very different situation from one in which high entry rates to the most prestigious universities created their own reality for subsequent students. There were also more tangible mechanisms. Anthony Jolly (Cathedral College) recalled that he and his fellow historians were 'all assigned to colleges to make sure we didn't double apply . . . it was all very well worked out', while Luke Michaels from the same school was coached at the last minute on how to get through his interview:

> I submitted a form. I rang up and got a form for the choral thing, I'd only applied to one college . . . I don't know I seemed to land on my feet. I just applied and got a note back saying 'yeah we'll audition you'. So I worked very hard on my audition pieces and things . . . I had a manic weekend writing essays and sent them off and then had a one to one cramming session with a rather whacko teacher who told me a few really killer points to say – one of which was a peach and stunned my subsequent Director of Studies . . . In the interview [he] said, 'Tell me something I don't know about Shakespeare'. So I did. I mean it wasn't my idea. I didn't know anything and if he'd really probed me about it I wouldn't know what to say but . . . it was something to do with the *Tempest* and I said, 'Prospero was playing an early genetic creator so that he was making Caliban as a sub-human human and Miranda who was human a sort of goddess.' I think you've probably heard it before but he didn't quite expect a rather naive choral scholar perhaps to come out with anything like that because choral scholars aren't known for intelligence.

Andrew Rider from Nortown Grammar guessed that his place at Oxford had owed a good deal to being at that school. He was offered a place after an interview, and reported that 'on the report they sent back to school they said apparently "Not academically outstanding but seems like a nice chap".'

It was not only the unique Oxbridge admission arrangements that placed private school students at an advantage. The schools also appeared to have succeeded in getting several relatively 'unqualified' individuals into other universities. Keiran Warwick (Bankside) remembered seeing a list of the entry grades of his year at Bristol University and being surprised that 'I actually had very low grades compared to the rest of the course.' Naomi Chandler (Dame Margaret's) got into Keele with just one D grade, and had a feeling that it was down to her headmistress: 'I think she might have written and said something, because I wrote to her for help.'

Choice of university study

Our privately schooled informants were not only more likely to have attended elite institutions. They were also more likely, as shown in Table 7.4, to have studied 'traditional' subjects. A relatively higher proportion of 'modern' and 'new vocational' programmes were offered by the former polytechnics, which were attended by a very much smaller number of former private school pupils. Even allowing for this, degree choices of students from the private sector were heavily skewed towards what we have called 'traditional vocational' degrees, of which law and medicine are the prime exemplars. Those from grammar schools showed an even stronger 'academic'

Table 7.4 Type of course studied by school type (%)

	Traditional academic	Traditional vocational	Modern studies	New vocational
Private	59.6	22.2	7.9	10.3
Grammar	62.0	20.7	6.9	10.3
Comprehensive	37.4	31.8	10.3	20.6
All	50.8	26.0	8.8	14.5

Traditional academic: established disciplines (e.g. maths, languages, history) studied singly or in pairs. Traditional vocational: programmes constituting or leading directly to long established professional qualifications (e.g. law, medicine, engineering). Modern studies: combinations relating to newly established fields of enquiry (e.g. media studies, communication studies, environmental studies). Modern vocational: 'applied' courses that have emerged more recently, either in recognition of new occupations or as an upgrading of professional training (e.g. catering, nursing, marketing, sports science).

and 'traditional' bias, while comprehensive school pupils were markedly less 'academic' and less 'traditional' in their choices.

These figures need to be placed in context because they raise interesting questions about the contents of elite education. We described in Chapter 4 the predominance of the traditionally academic and specialized A-level quali-fication over any vocational alternatives. This has survived despite calls for programmes that better fit the demands of 'modern' employment – notably, flexibility in crossing disciplinary boundaries and greater emphasis on applying academic knowledge to practical problems. But as we noted then, criticism of the economic irrelevance of a 'liberal' education ignores its significance in marking social distinctions and its continuing high market value in 'meriting' access to a wide range of professional and also of mana-gerial employment. Although even elite private schools have participated in the shift towards some career-oriented subjects, notably computer studies, this has occurred within a curriculum at school level that remains strongly classified and 'academic' in largely traditional terms (Edwards 1997).

At the next stage, and although a 'new vocationalism' has emerged from its historical confinement to those 'destined' for at best intermediate levels of employment, the market value of traditional credentials has been main-tained in elite institutions with highly selected intakes (Bernstein 1996: 86–8). This is despite the growth, accelerating since our informants were students, in areas (or 'regions') of knowledge formed by amalgamating old disciplines with new technologies (biotechnology, for example), or discard-ing them in favour of practice-oriented 'studies' such as management. Bourdieu (1998) described the latter as offering 'educational sanctuaries' to economically advantaged students relatively low in cultural capital and in prior achievement. However, as a survey of recruitment to high-paying City law firms showed, preference is still likely to be given to those with degrees in traditional subjects from 'good' universities (*Times Higher Educational Supplement* 14 July 2000). These continue to be taken as the best proxy measures of 'natural' and transferable abilities (Brown and Scase 1994; Bynner 1999). What Bourdieu (1998: 150) called 'specialists in the general' are still ranked above the technical specialists whose activities they will later manage.

In relation to access to universities, as we have noted, there was less indication of gender differences in our cohort than in other studies. Males were somewhat more likely to have attended the highest-status universities than females with equivalent entry qualifications. That the differences in our sample were small may be explained by the better academic perform-ance of the private sector girls and the explicit fostering of high ambitions in some of their schools. However, the predictable gender gap in degree subject studied was again evident. As in their choice of A-level subjects, boys had been far more likely to study science-based subjects at university, while the proportion of girls who studied arts or humanities was much greater. Over half the male students studied for a BSc or BEng compared with just under one-third of female students. The proportions for BA degrees were more or less reversed. The gender gap was once more apparent in the non-selective state sector, although our data suggest that the selective schools (all single-sex) were more successful in steering boys towards the arts subjects than in steering girls towards the sciences. Where only 15 per cent of comprehensive boys studied for a BA, this figure was doubled for boys at private schools, and doubled again to 60 per cent for boys at selective state schools. The figure of just over a third of girls studying science or engineering was constant across all school sectors.

There was no significant gender difference in the numbers who had studied the traditional vocational subjects, although relatively more women had studied law and relatively more men medicine. The latter difference was accounted for by male entrants from the unselective state sector, women medical students coming almost exclusively from the private sector. Although teacher training had traditionally diverted many academically able women from seeking a university place (Jackson and Marsden 1966; Crompton 1992), our cohort reflected the widening of opportunities in higher education since the 1970s. Teaching had been the vocational choice for only 13 out of 178 women (7.3 per cent), whether through a BEd degree or a postgraduate teaching qualification. The proportion was almost the same among the men, 13 out of 169, or 7.6 per cent. It may be that teaching is now a preferred career choice for women from a lower socio-economic background.

Progress at university

Most of our respondents' educational careers had been focused on 'getting there' – and most did indeed arrive at university. Many recall their university careers as the most significant time of their lives and many revelled in the new-found freedoms of being away from the constraints of home and school. However, for others, these freedoms created problems as they moved away from highly structured environments and relatively closed social circles.

Some had trouble adapting to different kinds of work regimes. Natalie Jackman (Highgrove) recalls how she met students at university, particularly from schools such as Nortown Grammar School, who seemed unable to cope with different kinds of demands.

> I don't agree with the way schools like Nortown Grammar are a bit like a sausage factory and churn out people for Oxbridge. I really don't agree with that. There's a lot of people who go to schools like that and get to Oxbridge, and they can't cope when they get there – I've met these people – because their education's been manufactured,

they've been spoon-fed so that they can't think on their own two feet. So I think it's a balance between being pushed and stretched.

Edward Hawksley, who actually went to Nortown Grammar, remembers the difficulties in getting to grips with what was required of him at Liverpool University:

> I was very sort of disappointed in university because you don't have the same sort of pressure at all, I mean you're supposed to create it yourself, and I was sort of expecting the teachers to come down on us ... I mean they aren't even teachers, the tutors ... I was expecting the tutors to kind of give us the same kind of pressure that we got at school. And ... I mean I actually did try at university to ... sort of put myself back into the school situation and I remember thinking in tutorials, that I was being far too kind of, aggressive, and competitive, and arguing too much, which was what we did at school, we used to, you know, all boys together, it was all sort of, 'Me sir!' and people would compete ... and you'd try and shoot other people down ... and it's not the same at university, you know you've got these girls there for a start who don't behave like that, and for English, quite a lot of tutorials, I'd be the only boy there, apart from the tutor ... usually, and I'd be there, sort of putting my hand up, and saying everything, and everyone would be saying 'Well, what's wrong with him? You know, he's being all kind of aggressive.'

Adrian Shakespeare had always found excelling at Cathedral College relatively easy, but floundered when he went to Cambridge:

> I discovered that there were moments when I just didn't know what it took to get a first. It was a very odd feeling. I felt I had done some really good stuff but didn't get the right marks. But, at the same time, I feel that I've underachieved ... everybody probably feels the same, and I've done other things too. But I've never been under pressure; I never thought that I'd get less than a 2:1 at university, for example.

Others found their new social worlds problematic. Brown and Scase (1994) talk of the relative ease with which the middle-class students fitted into the social worlds of Oxbridge and home counties universities. The issue though is more accurately related to the nature of the middle-class assets that are held. Middle-class children from backgrounds based on entrepreneurial and organizational assets could feel as much a 'fish out of water' as working-class students.

> I wouldn't choose Durham again. Well I chose it purely because it was considered the next best university but it was full of people from private schools and it's just completely different. They were amazing these people. They all had dads who were head of maths and they'd all been

through private school, and had their little cliques and not my thing really.

(Jackie Henries, Highgrove County, father, computer operator)

I think the first obvious mistake which really made me unhappy was leaving school and going to Durham University and joining a particular college which I did . . . although I came from grammar school, it is not really quite the same thing as a boarding school. And I am surrounded by these people who are very confident at that age, a little bit arrogant possibly and I found it very, very difficult to integrate into a college like that.

(Michael Judkins, Nortown Grammar, father, senior manager)

Even students such as Sian Allan (Moorside), who came from a professional background (her father was a vicar) but had relatively little experience of moving in such culturally privileged circles, struggled to fit in: 'I felt so, utterly contemptible and scorned that I didn't . . . partly I didn't dare relate to them, because they were sort of socially up there and I was just a worm.'

Middle-class students from comprehensives often reported differences between themselves and their colleagues from private schools that made it difficult for them to feel that they 'belonged' at elite universities, as the following accounts of life at Durham indicate:

I was almost intimidated when I first got there by the confidence of these people. And that's coming from someone who's not exactly a shrinking violet themselves. And it was intimidating, at first. But what was interesting was the nature of their confidence, which tended to have been very loud and very up-front, very self-assured.

(Lara Button, Shirebrook)

I think they're better at presenting themselves and they tend to be better spoken. At Durham there was always a bit of mickey-taking about my accent. We used to argue about how to say certain words – like Newcaarstle! They [ex-private school students] seemed a lot more positive and outgoing – they tended to be more forthcoming.

(Isaac Cordell, Frampton)

Andrew Rider (Nortown Grammar), the son of an optician, had similar problems:

I think when I got to college, before I went to Oxford, it was nice to think that I was going somewhere really prestigious and full of people from jolly good schools and they were all jolly good, but I just didn't find that I fitted in there . . . on this superficial basis, I thought that it was all a bit 'Ya'.

About half of our respondents came from the north of England, and had regional accents even when they had 'solidly' middle-class backgrounds. Several commented on how this singled them out 'down south'. Annette Silver (Highgrove County), for instance, remembers:

> You know they say things like 'Gosh aren't you really northern?' And it had never occurred to me before because when you're out say in Nortown people think you're so posh – because you're from Highgrove, you're so posh. And of course when you get down to Oxford then they think you're northern and common.

Sarah Kemsley (Milltown High) remembers her shock when she arrived at Bristol University:

> I mean I had the wrong accent, I had the wrong clothes, I had the wrong hair. Very much more money-oriented. I knew it had a good reputation but for me the good reputation, money, didn't mean the same thing. I hadn't worked that one out yet. Neither had I appreciated how strong my northern accent is and that's hard.

Many accounts of differences between universities draw out contrasts between those at opposite ends of the status hierarchy. Ainley (1994), for instance, contrasts the student populations of 'home counties' and 'inner city' universities in terms of their socio-economic background and the social circles in which they move. However, our sample were attuned to more subtle differences, not just between elite universities, but even between colleges *within* them – reflecting the complicated and differentiated nature of the English middle classes and the endless variety of 'social types' that the education system is capable of producing and reproducing.

Faith Kennedy (Dame Margaret's), for instance, was sensitive to the differences between course populations:

> I mean when I went to university I did history of art which was . . . the Sloane subject and it was like the Sloaney division and almost everyone of them who did history of art in my year had gone to private schools and we were always the ones who lived in London and had the cars and it puts other students off you – not that you go out of your way . . . but we were student students if you know what I mean.

Interruptions and sideways movements

More than half of our interview respondents had some form of 'troubled' or 'broken' progression from school to the successful completion of their first degree course. Of course, a 'break' in progression is not necessarily a sign of a 'damaged' career. As Ball *et al.* (2000) and Du Bois-Reymond

(1998) point out, middle-class youth can enjoy an extended transition from adolescence to independent adulthood – perhaps best exemplified by the increasing use of a 'gap year'. However, it would be difficult to describe many of our respondents' 'interruptions' and 'diversions' in getting to and progressing through university as anything other than problematic for them. In addition to changing and retaking A-level courses, many students shifted degree courses and universities. Some students felt they had taken the wrong course in the first place, some were unhappy with the location of their universities and wanted to move closer to home or to new-found partners. Karen Nixon's (Dame Margaret's) account is typical of those with very disrupted, but ultimately 'successful', higher education careers:

> I started doing French with European studies and then in my third year, I went to Toulouse for a year and came back and I then withdrew just before my finals and took a year and a bit out . . . I was ill, I had a break down so a lot of, well a lot of it was recovering and then when I was starting feeling a bit better . . . I stayed with my parents and then went back the following autumn to try and go back to college and I did actually drop out again. Then I stayed up in Edinburgh and started doing voluntary work and I did that for a year and then went back to college . . . I went back and repeated the final year but just doing single honours French . . . I wasn't too clear I wanted to get my degree, but it was more the fact of having a degree than anything else . . . I knew I'd made the wrong choice of what I'd studied . . . I did consider going right back to A-levels and doing it [medicine] but I don't know, it would've been a very long process.

In the end, the majority of our students who started degrees finished them – even if not on the original course that they had started. Although the graduates from private schools included a slightly higher proportion with 'firsts' than those from comprehensive schools (10 per cent compared with 7 per cent), the distribution of degree classifications generally did not vary significantly between the sectors. Such comparisons are not particularly useful when 62 per cent of those classified are in the conventional 'good honours' categories (with another 32 per cent 'lower seconds') and when a higher qualification from one institution may be less marketable than an apparently inferior performance from another.

And then on to further study

Although a slightly higher proportion of our women than men informants had gained a university degree, the degree classifications themselves showed no significant gender distinction. However, as the numbers of graduates have increased, so too in a competitive job market the value of postgraduate qualifications has increased. Forty-four per cent of the graduates in our cohort had progressed to postgraduate study of some kind, either higher degrees or professional/vocational qualifications, such as law, medicine or languages, although a third of these were still in the process of completing their courses at the time of our research. The pattern here again indicated that women graduates were more likely to undertake some further study following a first degree (48 per cent, compared with 38 per cent of men), but it was the women from selective schools, particularly from the private sector, who were most likely to follow this route. Forty-eight per cent of these women from private schools had already obtained a postgraduate qualification at the time of our research, with a further 9 per cent in the process of completing a course, making a total of 57 per cent who had embarked on or continued with study beyond the first degree. The comparable figures for men from private schools were 29 and 12 per cent respectively.

Those who carry on from sixth form or further education to college to their first degree and then to postgraduate study can be seen as having extended and successful educational careers. In the next chapter, we look at those who can be characterized as educational 'failures' rather than 'successes' – even if the definition of failure is somewhat at odds with conventional understandings of the term.

Note

1 Our ranking of universities was adapted from the 'performance' and 'reputation' tables regularly published in the media, which are largely consistent in their placing of institutions. For most purposes, we use three broad categories: Rank 1, Oxbridge and other élite 'old' (pre-1992) universities; rank 2, other 'old' universities; rank 3, 'new' (post-1992) universities (including ex-polytechnics), colleges of higher education (CHEs) and other local colleges.

 **8** Failing against the odds?

The dominant emphasis within the sociology of education is generally on cultural *re*production, on how generations and institutions preserve rather than interrupt privileges. This emphasis often ignores the extent to which there is discontinuity in the processes of social and cultural inheritance. Downward social mobility has fluctuated in recent years, but even in the 1980s, which are widely seen to be a period of middle-class expansion, there were significant amounts of downward movement. Fielding (1995) claimed that in the ten years between 1981 and 1991, 21 per cent of managers and 14 per cent of professionals had experienced downward mobility into manual or routine white-collar work or unemployment. In that context, the impact of changes in parents' socio-economic status on their children's educational careers has focused largely on intensified motivation to restore family fortunes through educational success in the next generation. It was notable, for example, that more than a third of Jackson and Marsden's (1966) 'working-class' families were identified as 'sunken middle-class', and that assisted places had particular appeal for parents educated 'above' their current occupation and income (Edwards *et al.* 1989). We also noted Saunders' (1996) conclusion that private schooling retained a considerable capacity to protect even less than academic middle-class children from the risks of downward mobility. As described in Chapter 9, those risks were already being seen more clearly in the late 1980s because of rising levels of middle-class unemployment and anxieties about increasing job insecurity.

These changes increased the value of the 'transportable' cultural assets embodied in education credentials compared with those organizational assets which tied careers to progress within the same employing organization.

In describing the overall profile of educational achievement within our cohort, and examining how this differed according to school type, we concentrated largely on 'success'. In this chapter, we explore some of the biographies of those who appear to have failed 'against the odds'. Perceptions of educational failure among our cohort of academically able and often privileged young people were, of course, highly relative. Conventional measures might include achievements below the national average. But although we look at the very few informants who failed by that criterion, they reveal very little about the expectations of educational success that surround middle-class children in general and able students in particular. In view of the overall rise in levels of educational qualifications between the generations, those who 'failed' to match their parents' level of education could be regarded as exceptional. However, there were many other respondents who 'succeeded' relative to their parents and their contemporaries, but who recount their own educational careers as being marked by failure. We therefore consider their experience of failure relative to their own or their school's aspirations.

Failure relative to contemporary national standards

Analysis of the British Cohort Study data for those born in 1970 and contemporary with our own respondents showed that 6 per cent of 26-year-olds had no qualifications, 17 per cent had Certificate of Secondary Education passes at grades lower than counted as equivalent to ordinary level and 41 per cent had at least one qualification at that level. Only 12 (3.5 per cent) of our own respondents obtained fewer than the five 'good' O-level grades, which we described in Chapter 4 as the threshold qualification for those seeking middle-class employment. None of these obtained no qualifications at all.

The 12 respondents (eight male) who achieved fewer than five O-levels/ GCSEs attended seven different schools. Four attended state comprehensives, one went to a state grammar school and two attended private schools. Nearly all expressed regrets at not having worked harder or gained more qualifications, especially the more vocational qualifications, which were not available at most of the schools in our study or which 'able' students would have been strongly discouraged from taking. They did not, however, convey a strong sense of personal failure in their accounts. In part, this may be because most of them seemed to have enjoyed active participation in sports while at school: football and hockey at the comprehensive schools, fencing, chess and rowing at the private and grammar schools. In part, it also reflected a lack of educational inheritance and aspiration. Although nine of the 12 came from 'non-manual' backgrounds, two had fathers in routine white-collar work and five came from 'non-professional' middle-class families. These parents tended to be small proprietors or managers without higher educational qualifications themselves. When we interviewed their children in the early years of their secondary education, only two expressed any strong interest in going on to higher education. Louise Boot (Parkside) had wanted to study science to be a vet, and John Hawdon (Rowton) planned to go to a polytechnic to be a probation officer. Others either had no intention of going to university or seemed to regard that route as a second best option. Patrick Elamine (Frampton) said he might consider a university 'if I can't get a job', and Nigel Borrie (Nortown Grammar) if he was 'not in the Army' by then. Only one of these students' parents had higher educational qualifications. Patrick Elamine's sister had gone to university, but this proved for him something of a disincentive:

> She was the first one in our family to go to university. I think I've used her as a bit of an excuse. There was always pressure from some teachers at school because Dawn had been so bright. She took some of her O-levels a year early, then took several of them again because she didn't quite like the grades that she got! So it was a bit hard sometimes, living in her shadow. Me mum and dad used to say, never mind what the teachers say. They didn't make comparisons. Fortunately for me, I excelled at sport. So I was more happy to concentrate on the sport. And I didn't think my work would suffer. But obviously it did, because I didn't get the grades – not only that I expected, but that other people expected me to get. I was quite devastated to be honest, when the results came and I'd got just those two passes.

In general, those with the lowest levels of educational inheritance did best in the private sector, but *only* if they survived past 16. In our sample, the eight assisted place holders from manual backgrounds who stayed at their schools beyond 16 progressed to higher education, all but one of them to elite or second rank universities. On the other hand, the other four of the original 12 had finished full-time education at 16, compared with only five out of the 32 from equivalent backgrounds at comprehensive schools. This would suggest that, while there are benefits of being 'sponsored' into academically pressurized environments, there are also risks.

Failing relative to parents

As argued elsewhere (Power 2000), children of parents with cultural 'assets' and/or those working in the field of symbolic productions are likely in general to attain higher educational qualifications than those whose parents

Table 8.1   Students' qualifications relative to those of their parents

Respondent's highest qualification	Father's highest qualification			
	O-level or less	A-level or equivalent	HE or equivalent	Total
O-level/GCSE or less	14	*4*	*4*	22
	(16%)	*(9%)*	*(3%)*	(8%)
A-level or equivalent	7	7	*10*	24
	(8%)	(15%)	*(6%)*	(8%)
HE or equivalent	69	36	142	247
	(77%)	(77%)	(91%)	(84%)

	Mother's highest qualification			
	O-level or less	A-level or equivalent	HE or equivalent	Total
O-level/GCSE or less	15	*3*	*2*	20
	(12%)	*(6%)*	*(2%)*	(7%)
A-level or equivalent	13	8	*7*	28
	(10%)	(16%)	*(6%)*	(9%)
HE or equivalent	102	40	112	254
	(79%)	(78%)	(93%)	(84%)

Note: Numbers in bold italics indicate students with lower qualifications than their fathers or mothers.

held property or organizational assets and/or worked in the field of economic production. But in comparing our cohort's educational qualifications with those of their parents, we identified a small minority who had not been able, or had not chosen, to translate their apparent cultural inheritance into educational qualifications.

As Table 8.1 shows, the great majority of our respondents at least matched their parents' level of qualification, and most had exceeded it. Only 18 respondents (indicated in bold) achieved lower qualifications than their father, and 12 lower qualifications than their mother. The apparent impact of a strong educational inheritance is even more marked when *both* parents' qualifications are taken into account. Of those students both of whose parents had higher education, only one obtained nothing higher than GCSEs and only another four nothing above A-level, and each of these obtained at least two A-levels.

There is of course no simple explanation for why these individuals had not 'lived up to' their educational inheritance. As we indicated in Chapters 5 and 6, educational careers are the outcome of a complex interaction between home, school and peer networks (see also Power *et al.* 1998b). In some cases, it seemed as though parents' academic abilities daunted their children by presenting 'a hard act to follow'. Rather like Patrick Elamine's recollection of being discouraged by his sister's success, William Jowitt (Archbishop Ambrose), who had achieved fewer than five 'good passes' at O-level, clearly felt somewhat daunted by 'an extremely brainy dad . . . He's got an alphabet after his name.'

Students who came from a background in which one or both parents had a degree expressed a far stronger sense of themselves as having 'failed'. As we discussed in Chapter 5, the high expectations placed upon them by their parents, themselves and their schools can lead to these students becoming 'estranged'. In particular, the strong academic hierarchy within some select-ive schools had sometimes proved demotivating. Adrian Slocombe had ambitions to be a vet when we interviewed him shortly after he started at Archbishop Ambrose. Looking back on his school career, he believed that its highly visible ranking of academic achievement had damaged his chances:

> To be honest if I had the time again, I would prefer to go to a different school and the only reason I say that is because a lot of people I know who didn't go to a selective school or a grammar school did better because they weren't made to feel so much under pressure. If I only had gone to a [comprehensive] school, then I would probably have found it a bit easier. In as much as I would probably have been in, say, the top ranks of the class rather than middle rank or whatever it was . . . And that's something that has been echoed by a lot of people I went to school with, even the ones that did well.

Despite his assertion that the composition and the ethos of the school con-tributed to his relative failure (fewer than five higher-grade GCSEs), his sense of disappointment in himself was evident:

> You have three or four guys who are outstanding at every subject and they are like a figurehead for some of the teachers, 'Come on, so and so could do this, you should be able to get at least somewhere at least near it.' Which is very demoralizing, if you are doing your best at a particular subject and you can't . . . And I felt cheated in a way, it wasn't anyone else's fault but mine . . . Well eventually, because I didn't get my GCSEs, the right amount. They basically said 'No, we are not having you back' . . . they were very disappointed and they said 'Look, you got six Ds, you could make it six Bs easily without all that much more effort if you'd done your bloody revision.' And I felt ashamed really, very ashamed because I think really they are right . . . I . . . should have done much better than I did. And they knew it, then I think I failed them as well as I failed myself by not doing the work, not getting the results.

Very exceptionally, students with higher levels of educational inheritance may become 'detached' from the school – and in these cases their lack of objective success as measured in exam performance may not be experienced as failure at all. In these cases, the academic path was actively rejected for an alternative route. Matthew Pearson, who had a new middle-class background, with a father working in the media and an Austrian graduate mother, left Archbishop Ambrose at the age of 16, a rare occurrence at that school, with eight GCSEs. He had done so to concentrate on his computing interests:

> He [my father] bought me a Sinclair Spectrum and so when I was very young and I started to programme it . . . I left at 16 mainly because I had the opportunity to work for my father in his company. I didn't like exams and things and just wanted out . . . the teachers weren't keen on it – especially the computing teachers . . . although they knew I was going into a computing related job and they knew I would enjoy it. Around that time I was getting much more involved in computer programming at home but on a much more advanced level than we did at school . . . I was doing a lot of this programming in my spare time and consequently I didn't do as much revision as a lot of people would have for the GCSEs.

His lack of willingness was less to do with his *own* inability to do the work than with the *school's* inability to provide sufficiently demanding work:

> I knew computing was what I wanted to do but computer studies courses were complete rubbish, absolutely dreadful . . . completely beneath me but also I didn't believe that those were things I needed to do for what I wanted to do in computing. It's a lot, a real focus on history of computing and things, the Babbage computing machine and things and we were still learning about punch cards when we were sitting in a classroom using BBC Micros. It was very disparate and I just thought, I was writing things with, playing lots of sound and things flying around the screen, like computer games, while we were being taught really trivial stuff and I just knew that A-level it would be more of the same really. It just didn't interest me. I wanted to do things rather than study the theory of them.

It needs to be noted that Matthew Pearson's reflections on his lack of conventional educational success are exceptional. For the majority of our students who achieved less well than one might have expected, lack of conventional educational success indicated personal failure. This is so even when they had actually achieved what in other circumstances might be considered perfectly respectable results. This was particularly noticeable with those students who had high personal aspirations.

Failure relative to one's aspirations

In addition to those who failed relative to their contemporaries and their parents, there are many other respondents who would, by any objective comparison, be considered 'successes', but who appear to construct themselves as educational 'failures'. Although examples of this can be found in varying degrees across our sample of students, it is most marked in those who went to the academically selective schools and who had been surrounded by high and early expectations of successful academic careers. A common argument in defence of selective schools has centred on the benefits of bringing together children whose abilities and aspirations produce a strong 'press' for high achievement. The effects of consequent peer-group pressures have been seen as especially beneficial for clever children from educationally 'poor' homes. But those effects are not all positive, especially where pupils are further stratified by attainment.

How their school had marked off academically able students as 'special' featured in many of our respondents' comments on their own educational careers. This 'marking off' occurred not just through attending selective schools, but also by being identified as 'special' within them. Gordon Drainsfield remembers with some bitterness the process of fast-tracking at Archbishop Ambrose:

> In the third year we were streamed into what they call 'advanced' and 'normal' streams. And the advanced stream at the time took all the O-levels a year early – the whole lot. So that was obviously a very tough two years. That was too quick really . . . I think looking back I would rather have done it normally because the people that were in my class in the second year that went into the normal stream, ended up doing GCSEs . . . I think I got four As and four Bs. But a lot of my colleagues who did the GCSEs, all got As for the whole lot . . . But my biggest grievance was the fact that I ended up doing my A-levels a year early. Which meant that I don't think, I didn't do very well at my A-levels. I really underachieved and I ended up taking them again and ended up spending another year studying for the second time.

What is interesting within these reflections is that Drainsfield considered his four As and four Bs at O-level to be a disappointment because a 'lot' of his classmates got 'As for the whole lot'. The celebration and expectation of very high public examination grades set by some of the selective schools our respondents attended made what would have been considered solid results elsewhere a source of shame. Ralph Foxwell at Nortown Grammar achieved straight A grades at A-level, but still recalled:

> Well again, in the context of Nortown Grammar School, getting As at O-level and As at A-level . . . although you would be congratulated, no

one would say 'didn't he do well', because the day . . . I remember the day I got into Oxford, obviously this was rather exciting, but as I think the year I got into Oxford about 60 other boys did the same, no one says, 'Ralph Foxwell, didn't he do really well.' It's more a case of being extremely relieved that you weren't one of the ones they said, 'You never believe it, so and so didn't get in' or 'So and so failed his exams.' Again, when you meet the rest of the world, and obviously people you get to know who didn't do so well, you realize it was quite good.

Stewart Moore at Archbishop Ambrose reported some disappointment at the time at his nine GCSE grades: 'Looking back now, yes, that seems quite respectable but . . . I think to myself I should have done better.' Faith Kennedy considered the B and two Ds she received for her A-levels at Dame Margaret's to have been 'a complete failure'. Hugh Bassey, who described his educational career at Cathedral College as 'not being terribly success-ful' and himself as among the 'least able' in his year, obtained two Bs and a C at A-level; his failure to get three As 'automatically puts me into the bottom half of the group'. Nowhere are the high level of expectation and subsequent experiences of failure and disappointment more pronounced than among those who set their sights upon Oxbridge.

The Oxbridge disappointment

In Chapter 7, we looked at the proportions of students who went on to higher education, and particularly to the elite universities. Although the high proportion who went to elite universities might be considered impressive for the cohort as a whole, for those individuals who failed to 'make the grade' it can be experienced as personal failure.

When we asked our respondents in their early teens about their plans after they left school, a significant proportion (15 per cent) stated that they wanted to go to Oxford or Cambridge universities. There was clearly a school sector dimension to this (see Table 8.2).

Table 8.2 Early Oxbridge aspirants

School type	Oxbridge aspirants	Percentage of school type cohort
Comprehensive	6	4
Grammar	11	32
Private	36	21
Total	53	15

One-third of our grammar school informants and one in five of those from private schools had aspired to Oxbridge, compared with fewer than one in 25 of those at comprehensive schools. The differences between particular schools are even wider – not one from Rowton or Vicarage Road cited Oxbridge as a destination, whereas nearly one in two (44 per cent) from Archbishop Ambrose did so. Our interviews illustrated clearly the impact of self-selection on the very socially skewed entries to those universities. Such self-selection into and away from that rather esoteric competition for places clearly reflects family traditions, family perceptions of an appropriate and feasible aspiration and (as explained in Chapter 7) what can be strong school pressures to follow that route. The effect has been to produce a much lower ratio of applications to places than in many less conspicuously prestigious universities, as well as notoriously unrepresentative intakes. Although we discussed this in Chapter 7, we return to it here in the context of 'disappointment'.

Claiming an increasingly meritocratic entry to Oxford because the chances of those from state and private schools with 30 or more A-level points are approximately equal, Halsey and McCrum (2000) ignore the fact that the state school Oxbridge entrants are predominantly both middle class and from church schools or the remaining grammar schools. Comprehensive schools, which are at least nominally non-selective, currently constitute 85 per cent of secondary schools but provide only some 20 per cent of entrants to Oxford and Cambridge (Lampl 1999). The Sutton Trust, which Peter Lampl created, has attempted strenuously to 'open up elite education' at both school and university stages. Lampl regrets that Oxbridge has turned back to being 'something of a finishing school for the rich' compared with its relative openness to the talented irrespective of social background, which he attributes to the 1960s. However, the 'rich variety of regional accents' at Oxbridge at that time may have belonged to the products of schools like Manchester Grammar School and King Edward's Birmingham – which are provincial perhaps, but certainly not typical state schools.

As described in Chapter 7, a significant number of our respondents – 13 per cent of the entire cohort – had ended up at Oxford or Cambridge. However, the identities of the 15 per cent who had aspired to do so and the 13 per cent who had succeeded are not the same (see Table 8.3).

Although so many had been disappointed in their aspirations, some schools appeared to have been remarkably successful at sending significant proportions to the elite universities. As we saw in Chapter 7, their emphasis on getting students into Oxbridge was noted by pupils, even those for whom it was not a realistic or desirable objective. Karen Nixon (Dame Margaret's), for example, remembers how these students were singled out for extra attention: 'You know for them it was the Oxbridge cream which mattered and the fact that I got a place in university, that's all that mattered.' However, it was not just other students that suffered from the Oxbridge ambitions of

Table 8.3   Unsuccessful early Oxbridge aspirants

School type	Unsuccessful Oxbridge aspirants[a]	Percentage of 'unsuccessful' aspirants by school type
Comprehensive	5	83
Grammar	7	64
Private	23	64
Total	35	66

[a]When interviewed in early teens.

their schools; those that had been singled out and failed found the experience deeply distressing. Edward Hawksley remembers how at Nortown Grammar

> they put me in to do Oxford, and to me, at that time, that was the sort of . . . peak of everything, of education . . . when it happened, it was the most humiliating thing . . . They picked all the people in the room, and the teacher just said, 'Right, you and you, we think you're good enough to do Oxford', and everybody else isn't, basically, I mean in front of everyone. So there was the two of us, and then they actually de-selected the other character, which must have been even worse for him . . . and then we were all put in for Oxford . . . well there was about eight of us, in the end, who were supposed to be doing English in Oxford, and we all used to have extra lessons, and it was all lots of fun and everything.

Some explained their failure in terms of their A-level grades not being good enough. For others, it was the now notorious and controversial interview. Whatever its merits at enabling applicants to gain some sense of the university they are considering, it is a main site for scrutinizing both their personal style and those qualities, including 'institutionalized charisma', which admissions tutors may expect to find more reliably in schools of particular kinds (Brown 1995). The stipulation of an oral exposition of ability certainly provides occasions to assess what Bourdieu has consistently described as the prime qualification for entry to elite institutions – namely, the appearance of 'natural talent' rather than 'mere' diligence, and the display of a fluent 'ease' in relation to high-status knowledge (Bourdieu 1984, 1998). Although many of our students were culturally privileged, some had been unable at the interview stage to display the 'intellectual prowess' that will mark them off as suitable Oxbridge 'material'. Selina Webster (Highgrove County) recalled how she had failed to impress:

> In the sixth form the school mentioned to various people 'We think you should go for Oxford', and there were a little group of us, and I suppose I was one of those . . . I was quite happy, I'd read the prospectus

and thought, Oxford looks like a nice place to go, and . . . at the time, yeah, I was keen to go, it was a big disappointment . . . I went to the interview . . . I don't think I gave a very good performance in the interview, again with hindsight I probably . . . perhaps lack of confidence, and also I do remember saying how rubbish Seamus Heaney was, who was Professor of Poetry.

Lana Giblin (Dame Margaret's) and Brian Hogg (Bankside College) similarly reflected on how, despite encouragement, they could not shine at the interview:

> I could totally understand why; during my interview I could see that he was really trying to give me a chance to say something intelligent, it just never really came out. He was trying to make me think like an economist; he wrote back to the school afterwards and said that a year out would do me a lot of good and that I should apply again if I wanted to; hopefully something would develop in that year . . . I felt that I would always have been struggling at Cambridge, they're all so hyper intelligent and I'm not.
>
> (Lana Giblin)

> I don't know why. I've got a pretty good idea why. I did the exam mode entry, and I did obviously well enough in that to get to the interview, and I went to the interview, and I went to the maths interview, and I basically got an attack of nerves, and everything just went out the window. It had never happened to me before, actually, it was quite . . . and that made it even worse for me, I didn't know what was going on because I really panicked and I burbled . . . interview was a complete nightmare.
>
> (Brian Hogg)

Edward Hawksley (Nortown Grammar) claimed that, of a particular small group of potential applicants, only one had made it to Oxbridge in the end. The rest, he claimed, were 'found out':

> Basically we did all right in the exam, and we went down for interview, and were discovered and un-masked within minutes . . . I mean I'll never forget that interview. I just thought, 'Oh God, you know, there is more to being clever than I thought.' Which was all a bit depressing. And at that point I realized, suddenly realized that I wasn't part of the elect, as I'd always hoped.

The stigma of failure

Many of the 'failures' we have discussed here would seem like successes to others. However, their experiences have left long-lasting legacies of low self-esteem and guilt, and often resulted in damaged educational careers that some respondents had felt unable to revive. Tamsin Nee (St Hilda's) was doing a degree in her mid-twenties, but had needed help to restore her confidence:

> I actually went to a hypnotherapist about a year and a half ago about my maths because I'm doing a degree at the moment. I'm doing my finals in nine weeks, and I had this mental block about it. I know exactly because I worked through regression, sounds a bit weird but, I was regressed and it came out that when I was about 13 or 14, I was made to stand up in class and got something wrong and I've always had this big problem with it ever since. Which has always given me a problem with maths. But actually as it turned out I'm actually quite good at it, well since I work in a bank and that didn't quite dawn on me at the time. That bothered me a little bit but I think more of it was perhaps lack of confidence rather than anything else.

Sacha Butcher (Dame Margaret's) recalls the feeling of being 'not wanted' by her chosen universities:

> You don't realize when you're coping with the rejecting. I can see now how difficult it is to get into universities and how scarce the places are. But at the time when someone's telling you 'you'll be fine, you'll walk it' and then you come to the place of not being quite as wanted as you thought you were.

For the children of those parents who made heavy financial sacrifices to purchase a private education, failure can be particularly guilt-laden. Anthony O'Reilly (Bankside College) recalled that there was a shared view among sixth formers there that they sometimes wished they could 'pay our parents back for all the things they paid for'. And asked at interview whether she thought she had fulfilled her parents' hopes, Faith Kennedy (Dame Margaret's) responded:

> Oh, god I will start crying. I never admitted I hated Dame Margaret's, I never told them I used to cry every end of holidays and every end of half term and I just didn't want to disappoint them, so I never told them. I was too frightened to tell them, because my parents are very strict and I thought they would be very cross if I told them I didn't like it. So all my friends knew, but I never dared tell them and then I went to a tutorial college for a term because I didn't do that well. I went to Cromwell Tutors and that was quite expensive about £1,000 per subject and I didn't even do that great although being there was very good for me, I didn't do that well but . . . I remember hearing them say, discuss between themselves: 'What does she want to do History of Art for? That is just a nothingy subject – she is wasting her life and it will come to nothing' . . . I just have huge child guilt all the time.

Only a few respondents claimed that their parents had expressed verbal disappointment about their educational achievements. Most claimed that their parents expressed sentiments such as 'we're happy so long as you are', even though they felt they might secretly be disappointed. Trisha George (Dame Margaret's), however, had a father whose high expectations for her made him constantly anxious about her school performance, pressuring her to take particular subjects and then refusing to speak to her when she did badly in her A-levels:

> I was told I was good at maths and I ought to do it and if I didn't do well at maths it was because I was lazy, that sort of thing, so I did that and chemistry. I really only did because it went with the others, but really I shouldn't have done it. I wasn't that interested in it . . . since the age of I don't know I suppose about eight I suppose, I was told I was good at maths and I think it was pressure from my father as well that, he used to tell everybody at parents' evening what I wanted to do based on what he thought I was going to do, not myself. So I think that had a huge influence . . . then when I went to Dame Margaret's or because I was with other people that were also expected to be doing well I was no longer on top and my father didn't like that . . . I think I just gave up all round to be honest, which is awful really . . . I think this must have been at the end of the first year, he I think had been talking to one of the other parents and he was less than pleased with me because I hadn't done well, or my exam results weren't what he wanted them to be. Now I didn't know any different because I didn't know what standard they set at, it was only the first year I'd been there, so I just said, 'Oh you know I thought they were quite difficult.' He expected everybody else's results to be like mine or less, so when he spoke to another parent and found that their daughter had done better, it was then 'Well you obviously didn't work hard enough.' He labelled me as lazy I suppose and so I thought 'Well I might as well be hung for a sheep as a lamb' and that's the end of it I guess.

The inability to fulfil their own, as well as their parents', expectations could lead not only to a lowering of confidence and ambition, but also on occasions to the rejection of educational pathways entirely. Gordon Drainsfield's (Archbishop Ambrose) failure to make Cambridge led to him abandoning the idea of university altogether:

> I did actually apply to Cambridge for a choral scholarship . . . I didn't get in. My predicted grades weren't high enough, I was never a three As candidate and that's really what you need to be these days. So in fact I didn't go to university at all and I got a job instead . . . I had high aspirations myself, you know, Cambridge and so on. I think those aspirations were too high. The only reason that anyone at the school

thought I had a chance of Cambridge was because I had a very good singing voice. It was known that if someone at Cambridge liked your voice enough they would kind of stretch the entry qualifications a little bit, but not enough in my case. That ambition again of being called a scholar stayed with me throughout my life at school, up until I was 18, and I didn't actually get it in the end. I was very disillusioned with studying of that type. I hated it, in fact, I'd had enough . . . all the way through the school, my only ambition was to go to Cambridge and be a choral scholar. I didn't get it and I didn't want to do anything else.

Similar sentiments are expressed in Keith Andrew's (also Archbishop Ambrose) account of his own transition, which also indicates what Ball *et al.* (2000) identify as the phenomenon of 'learning fatigue':

I'd lost interest in education as a whole. I would have said . . . it was pretty much universal you applied to university. So I was told after I'd applied I should be applying for polytechnics as well. I hadn't and I took that as a bit of an added insult really. It didn't help my workload. I just thought, 'Well are you suggesting that I wouldn't get into university?' So I thought, 'Well you've given up on me, why should I put in any extra hours?'

These various accounts illustrate that, although 'failure' for middle-class children may be less visible and harder to quantify than for working-class children, it can perhaps be more traumatizing on an individual level. In the next chapters we explore more fully the linkage between educational achievement, occupation and social location. These data show that, while our middle-class students in general manage to sustain their socio-economic status, those with troubled and damaged educational identities can have difficulties in taking up the social positions that their cultural inheritance, educational pathway and academic ability seemed to promise. For some of our respondents, it was their early promise that appears to have been a factor in their 'downfall'. As Edward Hawksley identified, the 'real problem' with Nortown Grammar was that 'it was further to fall from . . . Failure from ordinary life is bad enough, but failing from such a high point makes it even worse, you know.'

In the next chapter, we examine the extent to which those of our respondents who are now unambiguously middle class have reproduced the social positioning of their parents.

Entering middle-class
employment

Substantial growth in 'middle-class' employment has significantly increased chances of upward social mobility as measured by changes in occupational status. It would therefore seem to have reduced the risks of downward mobility for those from middle-class origins. But Ball *et al.* (2002: 69) draw too sharp a contrast between middle-class concerns about 'staying as they are and who they are' and working-class concerns 'about being different people in different places'. The heterogeneity of the middle class and the rise of those 'new' fractions described earlier greatly complicate 'staying as they are'. And even in the past, as we noted earlier, the capacity of elite schools to convert 'new wealth into cultural assets for the next generation' (Scott 1991: 115) is only one example of a particular form of schooling facilitating movement within the middle class. In this chapter, we explore the extent to which those of our respondents who are now unambiguously middle class have reproduced the social positioning of their parents.

The middle-class recruits

In our earlier study (Edwards *et al.* 1989), we viewed 'middle-class employment' largely in Service Class terms. That large and diverse category is little used outside British sociology, and it has connotations of routine 'service' occupations which can be confusing. But it is useful in distinguishing professional, administrative and managerial workers from the self-employed and from other non-manual workers. It is 'a class of employees' (Goldthorpe 1995), differentiated partly by the extent to which access is dependent on education credentials, and therefore by the relative significance of economic and cultural assets in transmitting advantages to the next generation.

The educational upgrading of middle-class occupations described earlier has not been a straightforwardly linear process. The supply of middle-class jobs outpaced until quite recently the supply of applicants with high-level qualifications, thereby creating considerable 'room at the top' for less well qualified incomers. Sectors of employment have continued to differ in their preference for 'well educated' recruits, British managers, for example, being until recently less qualified than their French or German equivalents. Thus Payne (1987b: 128) has suggested that, while entry to professional employment has certainly become more closely tied to qualifications, academics whose own positions have depended on educational achievement have tended to over-generalize that link. If some caution is needed, there is no doubt that credentialism has become more pervasive, providing a mechanism for sifting applicants for desirable employment on apparently fair and efficient grounds. An apparent decline in 'lifelong' careers, and consequent anxieties about job insecurity, have also increased the value of 'transportable' credentials that are not locked in to a particular organization and can be carried from one employer to another. The most obvious are those qualifications from elite institutions likely to be taken by employers as reliable sources of general ability and desirable personal traits (Brown 1995; Robertson and Lauder 2001). As described in Chapter 7, the huge rise in participation in higher education has been both the cause and effect of its increased significance for entry to employment, and therefore of concern about unequal access to the upper reaches of a stratified system.

It was to be expected that our 'well educated' informants would have sought and secured professional, managerial and other non-routine white-collar jobs. Again, the large and educationally heterogeneous British Cohort Study provides useful comparisons. It shows, for example, how both employment rates and relative security of employment rose with level of qualification (Bynner 1999). Of our informants, 93 per cent of those in paid employment were in non-manual jobs at the time they were questioned, and 75 per cent in professional or managerial occupations; 23 per cent were not in paid employment, but that category included a range of activities from studying and writing up academic theses to taking time out in travelling the world. Of all BCS respondents, 40 per cent were in professional or managerial employment (classes I and II in Table 9.1).

In order to examine whether these differences provide evidence of movement out of or within the middle class, this chapter focuses particularly on those 199 respondents (comprising 75 per cent of the total cohort) who were already in classes I and II. The educational and occupational success

Table 9.1 Social class of our respondents

	No.	Percentage
Class I	68	25.7
Class II	131	49.4
Class III NM	47	17.7
Class III M	10	3.8
Class IV	8	3.0
Class V	1	0.4
Total	265	100.0

of our sample relative both to their contemporaries and to their own parents might appear to endorse Saunders' (1996) conclusion, from his analysis of earlier National Child Development Study data, that the British education system has become largely meritocratic. Critics of its inequalities, he argued, have been so preoccupied with a few elite enclaves with largely closed access that they have under-estimated the extent to which ability and effort are rewarded outside them. The overall profile of our own respondents' achievements, however, hides complexities that throw some light on changing patterns of movement within the middle class, and on ways in which educational and social differentiation is perpetuated or modified in a context of rapid growth in higher education and in middle-class employment.

Professional and managerial classes

We begin by returning to the within-class differences touched on in earlier chapters. Although most classificatory systems differentiate vertically between upper and lower levels of middle-class occupational status, horizontal differentiation based upon the ownership of distinctive types of asset are more useful for our purposes. Thus Savage *et al.* (1992) identify three distinct middle classes: the petite bourgeoisie or entrepreneurs holding property assets; managers holding organizational assets, which Mann (1993: 549) in a similar typology describes as 'careerists' moving up corporate and bureaucratic hierarchies; and professionals holding cultural capital and operating in collectively organized occupations licensed by the state. The first of these, the petite bourgeoisie, has been relatively unimportant in terms of class formation in Britain, but the divide between the managerial and professional classes is, they argue, fundamental to any understanding of the middle class. Our respondents in social classes I and II can be allocated to these three groupings as shown in Table 9.2.

Table 9.2   Distribution of professional and managerial occupations

	No.	Percentage
Professional	141	70.9
Managerial	57	28.6
Entrepreneurial	1	0.5
Total	199	100.0

Given that our respondents were selected on the basis of their own educational promise, and that the majority of their parents were also well
educated, it is not surprising that although over a quarter were in managerial positions, the majority have based their occupational status on the
cultural assets associated most closely with professional occupations.

Given other evidence that women are relatively more likely to seek the
transferable academic qualifications more common in professional work,
it was interesting that, although more of the women were in professional
(54 per cent) than in managerial (46 per cent) employment, the difference was
not statistically significant. This was in sharp contrast to their mothers, the
overwhelming majority of whom (over 80 per cent) were employed in professional positions. The contrast may reflect the growing success of women
in some traditionally male-dominated occupations, or it may reflect the
different ways in which female careers develop. Crompton (1992) argues
that professional occupations provide opportunities for women to operate
as 'practitioners' and reconcile the competing demands of work and family,
whereas managerial occupations tend to require 'careerists' who will find it
difficult to combine their upward progress within the organization with
dependent children.

As Table 9.3 shows, graduate qualifications were closely associated with
occupational status. This was clearest in relation to the women, among
whom there was markedly more polarization in terms of socio-economic
status (and earnings) than among the men.

Table 9.3   Social class of graduates (percentages)

	Male (n = 124)	Female (n = 141)
I	31.5	20.6
II	46.8	51.8
III NM	16.1	19.1
III M	4.0	3.5
IV	0.8	5.0
V	0.8	0.0

Excludes those with no paid employment.

Overall, our findings illustrated the continuing relative advantage enjoyed by men. Even in these early stages of their careers, when they were still only in their mid-twenties, Table 9.3 shows our male respondents to have been in slightly higher level jobs than the women with similar qualifications. Table 9.4 shows them to have been earning significantly higher salaries.

Table 9.4   Respondents' earnings (percentages)

	Male (n = 124)	Female (n = 139)
Up to £15,000	39.5	61.2
£15,000–30,000	57.3	35.7
£30,000+	3.2	2.7

Excludes those with no paid employment.

Table 9.5   Graduates' earnings and rank of higher-education institution (percentages)

	Rank 1		Rank 2		Rank 3	
	Men (n = 31)	Women (n = 34)	Men (n = 39)	Women (n = 50)	Men (n = 20)	Women (n = 23)
Up to £15,000	12.9	38.2	28.2	56.0	70.0	75.0
£15,000–30,000	80.6	55.9	66.7	44.0	30.0	25.0
£30,000+	6.5	5.9	5.1	0.0	0.0	0.0

This general pattern of gender differentiation was less evident among those who had been educated in the private sector, among whom there was greater parity. The potential benefits of high-status credentials were most apparent for graduates from 'top ranking' universities (see Table 9.5).

Our evidence suggests that the gendering of occupational opportunities is less marked at the upper levels of the labour market, especially in those professional occupations most closely tied to qualifications (Crompton and Sanderson 1990; Heath and Cheung 1996; Egerton 1997). Thus although male graduates earned somewhat more than their non-graduate male contemporaries, the differences were much larger between female graduates and non-graduates. That women have to rely relatively more than men on higher educational credentials in order to advance their occupational status and earnings is illustrated by the higher positioning of non-graduate males

Table 9.6 Social class of non-graduates (percentages)

	Male (n = 34)	Female (n = 27)
I	8.8	0.0
II	44.1	25.9
III NM	32.4	48.1
III M	11.8	11.1
IV	0.0	14.8
V	2.9	0.0

Excludes those with no paid employment.

Table 9.7 Earnings of non-graduates (percentages)

	Male (n = 34)	Female (n = 26)
Up to £15,000	58.8	88.5
£15,000–30,000	38.2	7.7
£30,000+	2.9	3.8

(Tables 9.6 and 9.7). More than half of the male non-graduates were in class I and II occupations compared with only one-quarter of the female non-graduates. Similarly, despite the traditional concentration of routine women's work within class III non-manual occupations, 26 per cent of female non-graduates were in manual work, compared with 15 per cent of male non-graduates.

In trying to ascertain what had drawn these young men and women towards either professional or managerial employment, we have examined parental background, school type and the qualifications they had obtained. The close association of parental socio-economic status and education with the educational achievements and occupational location of their children is well documented. It is also claimed (for example, by Fielding 1995) that it is relatively easier for professionals to pass on their advantages. This was not apparent in our evidence, which showed almost equal proportions from managerial and professional families already in classes I and II. There was a relationship, however, between the occupational grouping of our respondents and that of their parents. Nearly three-quarters (72 per cent) of those in professional occupations had professional fathers and over one-half (51 per cent) of those in managerial posts had 'manager' fathers. A similar pattern was evident in relation to their mothers' occupational grouping. Thus we have some evidence of professional and managerial status being 'inherited', but very little to suggest that professional or managerial parents are differently advantaged in their capacity to pass on their social status.

There was no clear relationship between the sector of school attended and occupational grouping. Rather more of those who went to private schools entered managerial posts than those who went to state schools (33 per cent as opposed to 23 per cent). The difference was not statistically significant, but as with other findings there were complex cross-cuttings in relation to gender. For instance, women who had been to private schools were three times more likely to enter professional than managerial occupations (77 per cent compared with 23 per cent). That this was not only a gendered preference is evident in the striking difference between state-educated and privately-educated males. The latter were almost evenly divided between professional and managerial occupations, but state-educated men overwhelmingly selected professional destinations (85 per cent compared with 15 per cent)

We see no obvious explanation for the preference for professional occupations among state-educated females, state-educated males and privately-schooled females. It may be that less privileged respondents (females) and those travelling less certain pathways (comprehensive schools) follow 'safer' credentialized routes into occupational success. Yet contrary to what might have been expected, the choice was not related to level of qualification. In A-level performance, for instance, rather more of those in professional occupations had passes adding up to more than 20 points, but the difference was small. And despite what might have been expected from earlier evidence of 'under-educated' managers (Erikson and Goldthorpe 1992), 86 per cent of the managers had degrees, compared with 92 per cent in professional jobs. The key factor associated with occupational grouping appears to have been the status of higher education establishment attended.

While more than twice as many of our graduates were in professional occupations as were in managerial ones, those who had been to an elite university were the *most* likely to be so. So while 40 per cent of those who attended new universities and colleges of higher education (CHEs) were in managerial posts, this was the case for only 14 per cent of those who had attended elite universities. If we look at the overall composition, over four-fifths of those in professional posts had been to elite or other 'old' universities (see Table 9.8). More specifically, fewer than one in seven of those who went to Oxbridge then progressed to a managerial position.

Table 9.8 Occupational grouping and higher education institution

	Professional	Managerial	Total
1. Elite	51 (86.4%)	8 (13.6%)	59
2. Other 'old'	55 (67.9%)	26 (32.1%)	81
3. 'New' and CHEs	26 (60.5%)	17 (39.5%)	43
Total	132 (72.1%)	51 (27.9%)	183

In a recent study of higher education entrants, those who chose the high-status universities and who tended strongly to come from high-status backgrounds were most likely to nominate a particular career route as the reason for their choice (Ball *et al.* 2002). This does not match our findings, which we place in the context of earlier discussion of the influence of schooling on occupational aspirations and of Hanlon's (1998) claim that there is a struggle under way to redefine the professions and to prioritize managerial and commercial issues within them. This might support Goldthorpe's (1995) contention that the boundary between professional and managerial classes has become more fluid. It may also be the case that the difference between professional and managerial employment is less one of kind than of level ('high' or 'low') within each.

While almost twice as many of our respondents were in 'low' as in 'high' level occupations, as would be expected of what was still entry-stage employment, virtually all of those in high levels were professionals (96 per cent). It is difficult to know how far this reflects a bias towards the professions in the way occupations are graded. Although levels were coded independently of the class I and II demarcations we have used elsewhere, it was difficult to distinguish 'high' and 'low' level managerial responsibilities with any confidence. The predominance of 'low' level managers may also connect with the different pace at which professional and managerial careers progress (Mills 1995). Those in 'low' level managerial occupations may find it easier to progress upwards to the higher level than those in 'low' level professional positions. Again, though, there may be the gender dimension noted earlier – that professions tend to offer rather more space for 'practitioners' than for 'careerists' (Crompton 1992).

We now return to the strong connection between the status of the university attended and current occupational level. Analysing links between higher education and Service Class employment, Marshall and his colleagues (1997) treated graduate qualifications as a single category (level 4) in order to use comparable data from different education systems. In doing so, they recognized that 'a more nuanced approach to the measurement of credentials' might have shown 'more of the variation in occupational destinations as being mediated by educational attainment, making it appear (for example) that children from Service Class families deserved their apparently disproportionate share of high status jobs by having done better "at the upper reaches of Level 4"' (Marshall *et al.* 1997: 136). Nuances defined in that way would not have helped our own analysis because 62 per cent of our graduate informants had obtained 'good' degrees, and there were no significant differences between them in the proportions doing so from the three main types of secondary schooling they had experienced. For reasons outlined in Chapter 7, where they had obtained their formally 'equivalent' qualifications was of potentially greater significance.

Our respondents who had gone to fee-paying schools were more than twice as likely to have gone to high-status universities. This cannot be attributed simply to A-level scores, although the generally close association between A-level grades and higher education destination does not support crude stereotyped notions of privileged connections and socially exclusive networking. Nevertheless, the five respondents who secured places in elite institutions with fewer than 19 A-level points had all gone to private schools, while six of the eight with over 20 points who went to less prestigious institutions came from the state sector. This is more likely to indicate self-selection in making 'appropriate' applications than deliberate institutional bias, and the strong direction towards the 'best' universities that many of our privately schooled respondents had experienced.

While the private schools appear to have been more successful at propelling their graduates into social classes I and II than the state schools, particularly the comprehensive schools, there is no clear school effect between those who have 'arrived' in terms of the level of occupation. In other words, school sector did not obviously appear to have influenced *level* of occupation beyond the association with qualifications gained. For instance, the relationship between A-level points and level of occupation is consistent across sectors. Of those in 'low' level positions, 16 per cent had nine or fewer A-level points, compared with only 3 per cent of those in 'high' level positions. Over half of those still in 'low' level occupational positions had more than 20 A-level points. But we have argued that even small differences in A-level points may translate into significantly different opportunities for higher education. It was the kind of higher education institution attended that appeared to have most bearing on occupational level, and to suggest again that 'the most culturally privileged' are disproportionately successful at getting into 'institutions capable of reinforcing their advantage' (Blackburn and Jarman 1993: 202).

The figures in Table 9.9 illustrate the increasing significance of going to the 'right' kind of university. Small differences in school performance may become magnified into significant differences in terms of level of occupation and be reflected in different earning power, particularly for those in the 'lower' level occupations (Table 9.10). Although the numbers are small, the effect of elite higher education is illustrated by the fact that none of

Table 9.9 Higher education institution attended and level of occupation

	High	Low	Total
1. Elite	31 (52.5%)	28 (47.5%)	59
2. Other 'old'	32 (39.5%)	49 (60.5%)	81
3. 'New' and CHEs	3 (7.0%)	40 (93.0%)	43

Table 9.10   Higher education institutions and salaries of 'low' level professionals or managers

	Rank 1	Rank 2	Rank 3	Total
Less than £15,000	9 (15.3%)	22 (37.3%)	28 (47.5%)	59
£15,000–25,000	17 (34.0%)	21 (42.0%)	2 (4.0%)	50
Over £25,000	2 (25.0%)	6 (75.0%)	0 (0%)	8

the Oxbridge graduates in managerial posts, but four in five of the managers from 'new' universities, were earning less than £15,000 at the time they were questioned.

Writing before the abolition of the binary system, Boys and Kirkland (1988) found little significant difference in earnings between graduate respondents in similar subjects but from different institutions. Since that time, the 'conversion' of polytechnics and the large rise in participation rates have, as discussed in Chapter 7, produced a hierarchy of institutions with very sharp contrasts in the social origins and entry qualifications of their students. Boys and Kirkland found it difficult to rank universities other than Oxford and Cambridge in terms of employer or employee preference, although polytechnic graduates were at greater risk of unemployment. Except that Oxbridge graduates earned higher incomes in most of the occupational categories they analysed, they concluded that subject studied was more influential than institution.

That finding is complicated by the interrelation of subject and university. Directly vocational degree programmes, and directly applicable knowledge and skills, have become increasingly prominent in the system at large, but the most prestigious institutions have been relatively 'protected' against moving far in those directions by the continuing employability of their 'academically' trained graduates (Bernstein 1996: 74). That prestige, and the market value of those programmes of study taken as the best indicators of 'general' ability, depend largely on how competitive entry to them is taken to be, and therefore on what is believed about the social and academic characteristics of their student populations. Bernstein's (1990, 1996) account of the 'regionalization' of knowledge in higher education therefore treats the survival of traditional academic disciplines as a special case.

His analyses of relationships between social class and pedagogy were premised on a fundamental distinction between the 'old' middle class, occupied in the production and distribution of material goods and services, and the 'new' middle class, occupied in the production and distribution of symbolic knowledge. In outlining the division of labour within those 'new' class fractions, he made a further distinction between those more and less independent of, or dependent on, the state.

The relationship between these various groupings – professional/managerial, public/private, symbolic/material – is complex (see Power 2000). While there were more professionals in the private sector than the public, there are proportionately more managers in the private sector. This pattern is reflected in connection with professionals' and managers' location within material and symbolic fields of production, although this does not mean that material and private and symbolic and public are synonymous or interchangeable. As might be expected in the aftermath of extensive privatization of industry in Britain, very few of those employed in the material field of production were in the public sector. However, over one-third of those in the symbolic field of production are in the private sector. In terms of our respondents, there is a gender difference in relation to the field of production. As one might anticipate, rather more women than men were employed in the symbolic field (56 per cent compared with 35 per cent). And, although more respondents were employed in the private sector overall, there was a higher proportion of women than men in the public sector (66 per cent compared with 34 per cent).

It is in connection with the demarcation between public and private that we can locate a significant difference in connection with school sector. There was an apparent association between sector of schooling and sector of employment (Table 9.11). Thus, while most respondents were working in the private sector, this was particularly so for those who had been to private schools. The difference was especially marked for women. Only 28 per cent of privately schooled females were in the public sector, compared with 53 per cent of state-educated females. It is important to note that this does not relate simply to level of employment. Two-thirds of those in both private and public sectors are classified as being in 'low' level occupations (67 and 66 per cent respectively), and one-third in each sector are deemed to be at 'high' levels (33 and 34 per cent).

Again, these findings need to be set in a wider context. We noted in Chapter 2 the appeal of the more academic public schools as entry to government service and to the 'higher' professions became more dependent on educationally certified 'merit'. Winchester was perhaps the most celebrated example, and it was also associated with seeking to instil in its pupils 'a

Table 9.11 School sector and employment sector

| Sector of employment | Sector of education | | Total |
	Private (n = 113)	Public (n = 81)	
Private	86 (63.7%)	49 (36.3%)	135
Public	27 (45.8%)	32 (54.2%)	59

marked preference for public service over profit-making' (Wilkinson 1964: 4). In that account, privilege entailed obligations to 'serve'. A more critical and familiar view is that the public schools diverted the sons of the business classes from following their fathers' occupations by inculcating a 'gentlemanly' culture which left them unfit for the demands of entrepreneurial life (Wiener 1981). That thesis was rejected entirely by Rubinstein (1993), who documented fairly high rates of recruitment into business. He also argued that it was financial services that had been central to Britain's economic success even while its reputation was as the 'workshop of the world', and that these had become an even more prominent area of employment. By the time our respondents were making their occupational choices, the academically successful products of private schooling were already showing a growing preference for careers in the City and the large corporations (Perkin 1989: 375). The declining attractiveness of erstwhile high-status public service professions is illustrated by Adonis and Pollard (1998: 93) who show a shift in initial career choices of Oxford graduates from a public service majority in the early 1970s to a huge private sector predominance by 1994. And the new 'super-class', as they describe it (1998: 67–8), is composed largely of those working in the City of London and in the private professions around it.

Our own respondents' occupational choices may partly reflect their parents' sector of employment, because whereas 65 per cent of fathers employed in the public (including voluntary) sector sent their sons or daughters to state-maintained schools, 58 per cent of fathers working in the private sector sent their children to private schools. Of our middle-class respondents, over half (56 per cent) of those working in the private sector also had fathers working in that sector, while over two-thirds of those in the public sector had fathers working in the public sector. There are indications here of those different orientations within the middle classes that we discussed earlier in relation to choice of school, with the boundary between professional and manager being less significant than that between public and private employment. There are some indications that the sector location of parents was translated into a preference for a particular education sector for their children, which is in turn reproduced in occupational location.

Some consequences are perhaps reflected in our respondents' voting behaviour and social attitudes. There was no difference in the proportions who had voted in the 1992 general election (Table 9.12) But as in the

Table 9.12 Employment sector and voting behaviour

	Conservative	Labour	Lib/Dem	Didn't vote
Private	44 (34.9%)	23 (18.3%)	23 (18.3%)	36 (28.6%)
Public	10 (17.2%)	18 (31.0%)	14 (24.1%)	16 (27.6%)

contemporary British Social Attitudes Survey (Heath and Savage 1995), there was a clearer 'left-wing' voting tendency among those employed in the public sector. Those in the private sector remained more oriented towards the party that has traditionally held up the importance of economic markets and of reducing state expenditure, twice as many of them (35 per cent) having voted Conservative. Those whose salaries depend on state expenditure are significantly more likely to support the parties that have traditionally emphasized welfare and government intervention.

Claims that 'left' sections of the middle class are likely to be among the main agents of further progressive or even radical social reform (Lash and Urry 1987) were not supported, however, by other indices of 'conservatism'. Compared to our sample as a whole, the respondents already in middle-class occupations were more likely to hold meritocratic perceptions of society and conservative values. Almost every one, irrespective of schooling, agreed with the questionnaire statement that 'if you're prepared to work hard it doesn't matter which school you go to'. They were also less likely to agree that 'in order to succeed in this society it's more a case of who you know not what you know'. This may suggest that differences within the middle class are superficial rather than deeply structured. Mann (1993: 570) claims that while blockages to upward mobility may 'unionize erstwhile careerists and mildly radicalize semiprofessionals', it is more likely that 'hierarchical mobility binds most of the middle class into upward disciplined loyalties'. Indeed, the recent decline in middle-class support for the Conservatives is a realignment more of political parties than of social class loyalties, the success of New Labour reflecting the conservative influence of the Service Class on British politics (Goldthorpe 1995: 324).

Conclusion

Although our findings can only be tentative, the data we have presented in this chapter suggest that schools may feed into the middle class from several directions. First, schools that are private and academically selective feed a greater proportion of their students into high-status universities and out into high-status occupations. In terms of *level* of occupation, however, the status of university seems more important than school sector, although the two were clearly connected. Despite some interesting gender differences in this respect, school sector did not appear to have influenced the choice of a managerial or professional career path. But schooling may contribute to horizontal differentiation of the middle class in terms of employment in the public or private sector, the selection of a private or state school reflecting a parental identification endorsed through choice of schooling.

If these tentative conclusions were supported by further research, they would suggest a relationship between school and occupational identity that extends beyond vertical differentiation within and between classes. The dimensions along which middle-class identities are constructed are complicated because they bring together factors relating to assets (professional, managerial or entrepreneurial), to field of production (material or symbolic) and to sector of employment (public or private). Recent changes in employment and welfare may well have already blurred the distinctions between these potential determinants. The struggle that Hanlon (1998) identified may produce more professionalized managers and more managerial professionals. Similarly, successive Conservative and New Labour policies have sought to bring public and private together in new ways and to increase the number of 'third sector' organizations. It is therefore difficult to predict whether current distinctions within the middle class are deep-rooted. Even if they are superficial and ephemeral, they suggest varying allegiances to private and public forms of educational provision that currently influence sectors of employment and political preferences.

 **10** The present and the future

In Chapter 9 we looked at some of the patterns of reproduction within and between different middle-class fractions. The picture was one of some fluidity, not least because of changes in the organization and ownership of industry and the rise of management. But there were also continuities between origins, pathways and current destinations. The high level of qualifications of our respondents has, in general, led to high-level occupations.

The close connection between academic ability, qualifications and middle-class occupations may suggest that our respondents are already launched on linear, and progressively upward, career paths. However, a theme running throughout our research has been the difference between the patterns of progress and how they are experienced. What looks like 'success' has sometimes felt like 'failure' and what seems to be 'upward movement' is experienced as 'drifting' and 'aimlessness'. When our respondents discussed their careers, it was clear that their work profiles were surrounded by uncertainty. Only a minority held clear visions of progressively upward career trajectories.

In this chapter, we look behind some of the patterns discussed in Chapter 9 and concentrate more on the personal narratives of how our respondents constructed their careers, in both the present and the future.

Just drifting

We have described most of our respondents as 'getting on', although at different rates of progress and along different pathways, albeit largely within the 'prime' trajectory. Some have 'got on' educationally, but were unable to translate their educational success into occupational success.

Edward Hawksley (Nortown Grammar), who, as we noted in Chapter 8, saw himself as an educational failure despite his degree from Liverpool University, now found himself without aspiration:

> I mean I came back from university and I haven't really done anything since. I've really run out of motivation completely. I don't think I ever really developed any motivation of my own, except negatively, and when ... at Nortown Grammar, it really was easy just to get swept through, in the tide ... and you wake up, washed up on the beach somewhere, a bit later after the flood, and OK you've got certain qualifications but you don't quite know how you got them, looking back on it, and ... you don't know what to do now. I never really, at any point, grew up to the extent where I could ... decide what to do next ... and that's why I stumbled around and then went to university without really knowing why, and after I left ... that's it, I didn't have a good enough degree to carry on. I didn't have a clue what to do at all. I mean, not a clue ... and so, I'm sort of stuck, really ... I keep hoping that I'll ... I mean, I don't know.

Sian Allen (Moorside) suffered similar lack of purpose, having returned from her degree in Cambridge to her home town:

> And then I still didn't know what I wanted to do, but I wanted to come back up north and live at home and be at home, because I have not been at home for so long, I had a real need to just touch base and not feel that it was going to be taken away from me which it had been several times during my college course. And so I just came back and went on the dole and carried on doing cultural work and conservation ... And I am a bit stuck now, because I still don't know what I want to do. Nortown seems to be quite a difficult place to find work which is ... If you are really ambitious and you know what you want to do, then go for it and succeed or fail, you've got a plan. But if you are not that ambitious, you want to work, but you don't want to work really hard or all the time and I don't, partly because I've still got catching up to do.

It is almost as if, for many of respondents, their objective was the credentialization rather than the ultimate occupational destination: 'I didn't do anything with my degree. I got a good degree and I was happy with that. I'd proved that I could do it' (Sian Trowbridge, Dame Margaret's).

For some, the lack of vocational direction within their careers created difficulties when entering the job market:

> I just felt that the degree I did didn't really direct you, it didn't really help you along...If you did engineering, you knew what you were going to do, whereas with biology you didn't know what you were going to do. It was here, there and everywhere – especially the environmental biology that I did. I thought the environment was going to be the big thing, the coming thing, but it didn't work out. If I'd gone into biochemistry or biotechnology, I'd be in employment now...I know a lot of people who graduated, and a lot of them aren't in employment either. Some of them are like me, working in offices.
>
> (Catherine Brunning, Rowton)

However, those who had taken the more vocational pathway felt that they might have done better with a more general non-vocational degree.

> When I started to do my degree places were crying out for law trainees. When I finished, it was completely the opposite and a lot of law firms had gone back to the old way of recruiting from only traditional universities. I think in terms of career possibilities I would have been better off with an English degree from a proper university, rather than a law degree from what was then a poly, now a 'new' university. I would have had to do more years to get to the stage that I was at already, but the view on applications is so different.
>
> (Amelia Otis, Parkside)

Amelia's experience endorses Boys and Kirkland's (1988) finding that in areas where university unemployment was greatest, polytechnic graduates suffered much higher rates of unemployment.

In general, though, and irrespective of the kind of qualifications obtained or current employment, many of our respondents had no clear idea of a future career.

> I always felt I didn't know what to do, what I wanted to do. And I still have problems thinking of what I want to do.
>
> (Barbara Nash, Vicarage Road)

> I've never really sat down and thought, people all throughout school and university people were trying to make you sit down and go what do you want to be doing in five years, what do you want to be doing in ten years, and I've always said I've no idea and I'll come to that when I get there and I'm still doing that I'm afraid, so I've no idea what I'm going to be doing.
>
> (Douglas Haworth, Nortown Grammar)

I'd be surprised if I'm still doing this job in five years. But, at the same time, I haven't the faintest idea what I would be doing.
(Pete Emerson, Archbishop Ambrose)

I have great difficulty deciding what I want to do in my future. I've always had difficulty in deciding. Sometimes I need things thrown in my lap and I just make do with what comes my way.
(Keith Andrews, Archbishop Ambrose)

Keith's 'making do with what comes my way' was reflected in other students' accounts of 'falling' into jobs, often by chance rather than design.

We had a party after my graduation, and I crashed out at a friend's house. And next day after clearing the house, she said, 'Right. Let's go into the careers department for a laugh and see what jobs aren't full.' And I said, 'Oh I'll come as well.' Because I didn't have any plans at all – I was just going to go on the dole, that's what my plans were. And I got the . . . what's it called, the graduate jobs thing. And I was just flicking through it when it caught my eye, 'Do you have a language degree and no job?' And I thought 'That's me.'
(Megan Jenner, Nortown High)

After I left university I spent a year temping and doing odd jobs because I couldn't find anything permanent, and then I literally fell into this job.
(Sian Trowbridge, Dame Margaret's)

Many thought of their current work situation as being only temporary. Typical comments from the questionnaire survey include:

I don't see myself doing this forever.

It's useful for picking up skills for something different in the future.

But at least I'm getting more cv experience.

For the time being it is quite handy, sort of slips in there, it is a bit of steady every week.

I don't mind it, it's not a terrible job, really, but it's not something I ever envisage being sat doing for the next 20 years or so.

Perhaps not surprisingly given the high expectations both held by and placed upon our respondents, the same theme of disappointment that many of them felt about their school careers is evident in their occupational careers. Occasionally, their disappointment relates to income and the feeling that they should have 'arrived' by now:

I always believed at this stage I would be something else . . . I think it is a lot down to the school. They always made us believe that we would have fabulous, fabulous pay. Even at university we were led to believe that you wouldn't accept the starting salary of less than £15,000. By the time you are 25, the world was your oyster. You know, I am still waiting for the starting salary. I just keep believing that I should be somewhere else, but I don't know which step I went wrong in getting there.

(Annie Paisley, Milltown High)

More often it relates to not feeling 'fulfilled' in their work:

It interests me at a low level. I don't really get that excited about my work. It would be nice to have a career that I could get excited about.

(Neil Gresham, Milltown Grammar)

I get on well with anybody, but it is not what I want to do, it doesn't really push me.

(Patrick Welcome, Moorside)

For some, the challenge and satisfaction they received from their educational success were not replicated in the workplace, something that caused some people to reappraise the value of their qualifications:

I've been successful in some ways, but I'm beginning to realize that I'm not so successful in other ways. I don't know if I'm comparing my measures of success with other people's. I'm reasonably contented with my life in general, but I'm not particularly contented with my career. But I think that, in terms of my education, I've been successful; in terms of my career, not so successful . . . I don't have such big ambitions, but there's nowhere I can go from where I am now; it's partly that. It's also the fact that I find the work tremendously boring. I don't think my particular skills are used in the best way. I haven't once used any knowledge that I gained from my degree. Although that doesn't bother me because I don't think now that if I had my choice again that I would do the same degree, if I would do a degree at all.

(Jeremy Bishop, Vicarage Road)

I feel frustrated. I think that I've got intelligence if I was in the right sort of job, but I still don't know what that is. I might even become a teacher; which is what everyone who doesn't know what to do becomes.

(Timothy Korecki, Archbishop Ambrose)

However, Cheryl Brook (Vicarage Road) and Matilda Cooper (Milltown High) both went into teaching and were similarly dissatisfied with their work: 'I have lots of doubts now. I'm thinking I've been doing it, this is my third year now. I think it might be time for a change' (Cheryl Brook, Vicarage Road). Matilda had applied to join the RAF:

I'm very disillusioned with it. I didn't expect that . . . It may be the school I'm at, I don't know but I won't know from the RAF until June which is after the resignation date so I'll have to make a decision and I think I'm going to leave the school.

Of course, it is not surprising that some of our respondents were unhappy with their current situation. However, as we discuss in the next section, if we look across the cohort as a whole, we see that this uncertainty, lack of clear design and intention to 'do something else' are by no means isolated incidents.

The redefinition of middle-class careers

As we have already mentioned, many of our respondents had no clear occupational strategy. Across the sample as a whole, 14 per cent (47) claimed that they did not know what they would be doing 'in five years' time'. In addition to these high levels of uncertainty, there was an even higher proportion who thought they would make multiple and sideways career shifts.

Multiple and sideways careers

Nearly one-quarter (23 per cent) claimed they would be doing 'something different' in five years' time. Sometimes, these were just general expectations that they wouldn't be doing what they were doing now, e.g.

Current job	In five years' time
Self-employed tree surgeon and fencing contractor	Not what I'm doing now.
Brand maintenance chemist	Not this job!! (Don't know)
Logistics manager	Anything except what I'm doing now.

Others, though, clearly aspired to a different career. In part, this is because some of them were doing work at a lower level than their qualifications merited while 'waiting' for something better to turn up. In other instances, though, their alternative shifts required significant retraining:

Current job	In five years' time
Primary school teacher	Either serving as an officer in the RAF or more music-based teaching.
Driver/general assistant	Being a practising psychologist.
Accounts assistant	Freelance archaeologist (specialist in human skeletal remains).
Public relations consultant	Member of Parliament/junior minister
Management trainee	If possible enter legal profession and be a solicitor.

This might suggest that, having found their academic careers more successful and satisfying than their work careers, a return to study was a welcome prospect rather than a necessary interlude:

> I feel very optimistic about the future, and I think, my only real horizon three years ago was to get a good qualification, that was of ultimate importance to me. This accountancy qualification, you know it's a professional qualification. I know I've got a degree, but I want a professional qualification, and it's a well regarded qualification, so really I set quite a narrow target really.
>
> (Daniel Brighten, Nortown Grammar)

Sixteen (5 per cent of the whole sample) looked forward to *two* changes of direction within ten years:

In five years' time	*In ten years' time*
Architecture/interior design project	Running my own card design business or having the opportunity to have some of my writing published.
Editorial work	Writing a biography of Thomas Hobbes.
My own business	Working as curator of marine mammals in an aquarium.

The emphasis on change may be related to the move away from the idea of a 'job for life' and the related uncertainties over the nature and security of many occupations. Roberts (2001: 57) claims that the data on workforce insecurity suggest that little has changed and the idea of workforce flexibility is 'largely the result of press scares and hype-books'. However, he also points to the fact that under 30-year-olds experience far more changes of status today than in the past. The emphasis on job insecurity, even if it is more imagined than real, is also connected to a shift in the way that people 'construct' their careers. Something of this shift is evident in Lewis Grimshaw's (Bankside College) comparison of his own feelings about work compared with those of his father:

> If I have a bad day at work my dad says 'Oh you've got another 40 years of that.' I'm not planning any major breaks but I'll probably be a bit disappointed if I look back in ten years' time and I've just gone through ten years of promotion. So hopefully something totally different.

On a more positive note, Chloe Carter (Vicarage Road) celebrates the possibility of multiple careers: 'I'm not thinking there's one thing I want to do in my life, I just think there's so much time, so much to do, there's lots of things I'd like to achieve.' These comments suggest what Savage (2000) refers to as the 'individualization' of the middle-class career. Rather than envisaging their careers as hierarchically staged, many of our respondents defined their work prospects as 'a project of the self', allowing individuals to pursue their own ' "life projects" in an environment offering them the resources and scope for self-development' (Savage 2000: 140).

Of course it could be argued that the lack of clear prospects or the aspiration of multiple careers is itself a middle-class 'luxury' rather than a response to the uncertainties of 'new times'. Ball *et al.*'s (2000) and Du Bois-Reymond's (1998) longitudinal research studies from England and the Netherlands respectively illustrate the extent to which the children of middle-class families are able to enjoy extended transitions with a 'certain nonchalance brought about by their social origin: they know that they are backed up by their parents' financial and cultural resources' (Du Bois-Reymond 1998: 71). One of our respondents considered her own decision to move into counselling after graduating to be 'early': 'I think I've really taken time to make the decision quite early on in my life really, most people don't decide what they really want to do until they're in their thirties or forties' (Olga Bundy, Highgrove County).

It is certainly the case that there was among the 'drifters' and 'switchers' little sense of urgency or financial need. And it is also the case that for some of our respondents, their relatively privileged social and school networks made the haphazardness of their career plans and the hope that 'something will fall into their lap' a realistic likelihood:

> Well basically when I was at university for the vacations I was work-ing for a company in the City and in my final year they said 'When you leave university you can have a job here when you want' . . . My brother's an aviation broker, for a rival broking house, and that's how I got the original contact.
>
> (Michael Stephens, Archbishop Ambrose)

> I went to work for Arthur Andersen, whom I work for now, for three months. That was arranged through the Careers Service, because one of the partners at Arthur Andersen had a son in my year at Cathedral College.
>
> (Lana Giblin, Dame Margaret's/Cathedral College)

Even for those without high-level qualifications, social contacts, personal capital and 'style' could open doors – something that Aggleton (1987) found among his culturally privileged but poorly qualified new middle-class stu-dents. As Tamsin Nee's (St Hilda's) account suggests, 'happening to bump into someone' can bring positive results:

> I happened to bump into someone, a kind of vague colleague . . . But I thought, I'm never going to get either the grade or the salary being a non-graduate . . . And my boss said if he hadn't known me for this job I wouldn't have got it. They wouldn't have short-listed me because even though I had experience I had no degree so they wouldn't have interviewed me.

Not all our respondents were complacent about their lack of success in the labour market. A few felt that they had either graduated or were looking for work at a very bad time. Annie Paisley (Milltown High) claims that the inflation of qualifications has put her in the dilemma of either accepting work at a lower rate of pay than her education merited or being squeezed out by new graduates:

> A lot of the jobs I have been offered, good jobs, have always been very low wages or very long hours. I mean, for instance, I was offered one six months ago with a great PR marketing firm but they said . . . the advert started off saying they wanted certain criteria and by the time we had all gone through numerous interviews, they were looking for a graduate with a 2:1 or above, etc., etc., and because they knew we were all desperate for jobs, they ended up offering us a £100 a week . . . it's not economically viable. And you could see their promises of, 'In 12 months, if you are doing well, we'll see.' Basically, they know that we are all so desperate for jobs, a lot of jobs that have been offered have been like that. They know how desperate we are and the older we get, with new graduates coming up behind us, we are prepared to work for less and less.

Linear and 'upwards' careers

Savage (2000) claims that the career as 'life project' is gaining ascendancy over conventional notions of middle-class careers in which employees could mark their upwards progress through incremental salary systems, gradual promotion and increased status markers. In this respect, it is worth noting that only one-third of our respondents (32 per cent) thought that they would be in broadly the same field after five years. Of these, 63 (18 per cent of the cohort) could be described as having mapped out 'upward' aspirations after five years. And only 30 of these (9 per cent of the whole sample) could be clearly described as 'careerists' in terms of having mapped out an upward career path in their field with different goals for five- and ten-year stages. Typical ten-year career 'plans' include:

Current job	In five years' time	In ten years' time
Actuarial trainee	Actuarial work at a senior supervising level.	High-level managerial work in the actuarial field.
Recruitment consultant	Same, but as manager.	Same, but as regional director.
Teacher	Still teaching: head of department or year.	Deputy head.
Assistant editor	Commissioning editor.	Editorial director.

| Running private dinners, conferences etc. | Something higher up within catering management. | Hotel manager. |

For 15 of these 'upward' planners, the goal after ten years was to be running their own company – something that was also mentioned as an aspiration by 14 of our respondents as a five-year expectation. Again, this reflects the shift towards individualized middle-class careers identified by Savage (2000). Although self-employment is seen as a stage in 'getting on', it disconnects the career from bureaucratic hierarchies and defines career advancement as being about 'proving yourself' (Savage 2000: 140). Becoming self-employed is therefore a much riskier strategy than organizational advancement. And should these individuals realize their ambition of 'going it alone', it may jeopardize their own and their children's future socio-economic status.

Related to this is the small but significant number of respondents who were planning to shift from professional to managerial work. Although most of our traditional 'professionals' were planning to stay within their field, nine had clear intentions of moving into 'management' responsibilities, particularly in accountancy and engineering. Again, this may have implications for future security. Fielding's (1995) analysis of Office for Population Censuses and Surveys longitudinal study data shows that organizational restructuring has made managerial careers 'riskier' than professional ones – with nearly one-quarter experiencing downward mobility between 1981 and 1991.

Twenty-one of our respondents had hoped to retire (two after just five years). Whether this is a fantasy or the extent of the belief in the 'enterprise culture' that was cultivated during the Thatcher years is impossible to gauge. Perhaps for some, like Matthew Pearson who left Archbishop Ambrose at 16 to develop his own software, the changing technologies have created new possibilities for self-determination beyond the traditional credentialized routes.

'Local' and 'cosmopolitan' careers

Jackson and Marsden (1966) explored in detail the social uprooting experienced by many of their able working-class informants whose schooling, and the middle-class occupations that followed it, had drawn them away culturally from their families of origin. This had sometimes carried a cost to their sense of personal identity. Upward social mobility had also entailed location away from Huddersfield for some. If our own informants moved 'away' culturally, it was because their education had created some distance from their parents, although many were emphatic about their continuing strong family ties. Carolyn Selby, for example, whose career at Milltown High School had taken her to considerable academic success and employment as an investment lawyer, maintained close weekly contact with her mother who had left school at 16. There may have been some tensions where children from 'old' middle-class families moved into the 'new' middle class, with its higher levels of cultural capital. For those children from 'managerial' backgrounds with low cultural inheritance, the sense of putting distance between oneself and one's parents is just as marked as for working-class children (e.g. Jackson and Marsden 1966). Craig French (Nortown Grammar) compares his social circle in Nortown with that in London:

> People have less conceptual conversations, they don't talk about things like ideas, they always talk about doing things. It is always like gossip and banter . . . My Dad is really . . . he doesn't read . . . he wasn't educated past 15, so I don't . . . I very rarely have more than ten minutes' conversation with him. And so, to a certain extent, I am just playing a role really and just being the good son, being the good son, getting on at work, kind of thing.

Often social and geographical mobility were interrelated, taking some informants not only away from their place of origin but perhaps towards more 'cosmopolitan' attitudes. A large-scale study of Canadian school leavers showed that the 'movers' among them showed higher career achievement and tended to come from middle-class homes, while the 'stayers' were of lower socio-economic status and lower educational achievement, and were less occupationally successful (Anisef et al. 1999). Disentangling cause and effect in those interrelationships would be difficult. In Britain, Fielding (1995) noted the high proportion of spatially mobile young adults in the professional class, and the particular significance of south-east England as what he termed an escalator region for the upwardly mobile. Middle-class professionals tend to be highly geographically mobile, with managers being more mobile than the petite bourgeoisie, but less mobile than professionals. Our data on place of residence are not sufficiently robust for us to undertake detailed analysis of the extent to which our respondents are more or less geographically mobile.[1] However, it is possible to identify distinctive 'cosmopolitan' and 'local' career paths, even among those who went on to higher education.

As we mentioned in Chapter 7, respondents with lower levels of cultural inheritance were more likely to have 'local careers', in that they often studied for degrees in nearby higher education institutions and were more likely to have found work in the region, in many cases still living with their parents. Even for some others from outside the south east of England, London was seen as some far away and distant place, while provincial towns and cities were seen to be more 'down-to-earth':

My choice of Newcastle University was significant, because my best friend went to Oxford. I mean, we're still friends but we've certainly gone our separate ways. Because I think Newcastle is such a down-to-earth university and Oxford is so not. And also living in Newcastle, it's like a northern town and all my friends who went to Oxford live in London. And I went to Newcastle and have stayed in Newcastle. And I think that's significant really. I think it's a very realistic kind of place to live – not all balls and tiaras!

(Olga Bundy, Highgrove County)

Sometimes there is regret over not having travelled 'down south':

I just wanted to be near Nortown. I don't want to incriminate myself because I am on tape. I just wanted to stay within the north of England and I wasn't really sophisticated enough to understand the potential that say, going to London, or going to an Oxbridge university would have ... I suppose, it would have improved my life chances ... My friend did the intelligent thing and got out and came to London.

(Cliff Todd, Nortown Grammar)

Daniel Brighten and Isaac Currie (both Nortown Grammar) were aware of the view that there were career costs of not working in London:

I'm not one of these people that's massively 'career at all costs', I couldn't go and work in London, I don't particularly like the lifestyle down there, I mean like I love going down and seeing my friends there, it's good, but I don't think I'd like to sort of be in the rat-race type of thing.

(Daniel Brighten)

I have no, I certainly don't have any desire to go back down to London. Perhaps I'd work outside of London. Other people say that you have to serve your time as it were in London if you want to achieve great things ... I've got one or two friends that have gone down to London because they want to speed up the career path I suppose but I think there is plenty of opportunity elsewhere.

(Isaac Currie)

Those educated in the private sector were generally less likely to be living with their parents, even when they were working in the same area, and half had moved away from their home region entirely. The south-east, and in particular London, was the occupational destination for many of those with 'cosmopolitan' careers. This endorses Fielding's (1995) assertion that the south-east of England is an 'escalator region'. His analysis shows not only that the region attracts large numbers of potentially upwardly mobile young people, but that they are promoted at rates 'distinctively above' those for England and Wales as a whole. Several of our respondents endorsed the importance of working in London:

But if, for example, I went back to Nortown I would be starting from square one; I have no contacts in Nortown for work. Whereas I've spent a year and a half building up at least a few contacts down here. And a lot of my social contacts are down here; I think I'd feel like a fish out of water if I went back to Nortown.

(Julie Rowntree, Nortown High)

I mean I really spent so much time outside of Milltown now since '89. I would say London is my home and Milltown is my origins, so I do still have soft spots for Milltown, but it is more of a case there is very little sort of in terms of employment to fit what I do or my education. Going into the family business is not an option I particularly considered.

(Richard Hemple, Milltown Grammar)

The distinction between 'north' and 'south' is not about employment prospects alone – it is also about 'moving on' to different social worlds. In general, university friendships were more important than school friendships for those with the more cosmopolitan careers, not least because the majority of their university (as opposed to school) colleagues gravitated towards London:

Yes, I mean most . . . the bulk of my friends in London are . . . Oxford graduates . . . people I knew there or people I've met through people I knew there who also tend to be Oxford graduates. I'd say about 75 per cent of my friends in London are either Oxford graduates or friends of Oxford graduates who I knew.

(Craig French, Nortown Grammar)

You go to Nortown Grammar, you almost inevitably want to go to university away from Nortown because you don't want to be in the same city, a lot of people are going to go to Oxbridge, London is a natural stop because certainly for the City now, you can't do it anywhere other than London. And most big companies are based around London. And again there's the interest of going to London.

(Ralph Foxwell, Nortown Grammar)

Where schools send significant proportions of each year group to Oxbridge and then on to London, links with old school friends could be maintained through 'old boy' circles in the capital:

We've kept in touch with about six or seven of them . . . but there are some obviously who moved say to London and things, we keep in touch with them . . . The majority of people that I know from Bankside who I was good friends with now live in London which is quite nice and I see them regularly.

(Morgan Comfort, Bankside College)

I sort of followed a group of friends and the majority of friends who also moved down to London and sort of did one of those . . . in account-ancy, advertising, management consultancy, banking and law. And they are all in this group, and they are all sort of working round the city and they all live very close to where I live. So it's a sort of herd mentality almost, my friends from college came down here. My friends from school don't live in Milltown either so there is no reason for that either.

(Richard Hemple, Milltown Grammar)

It is not just the work opportunities: there is a sense in which those who move on see themselves as more sophisticated than those they left behind – cosmopolitan rather than provincial or parochial.

And you begin to notice now . . . this is a sweeping statement, but, the ones who go back to Nortown are . . . not looked down upon, but it's an easy option. Big fish in a small pond syndrome. So virtually everyone I know since Nortown Grammar has come to London. And those who haven't, no one would say it to their face, but you think 'Why bother?'

(Ralph Foxwell, Nortown Grammar)

I'm not really in contact any more with anybody who still lives in Nortown which is a shame. Everyone I know is really scattered round the world.

(Douglas Haworth, Nortown Grammar)

Some thought on a global rather than a national scale. Harriet Barrett (Highgrove County), for instance, wants to be a lecturer in an 'excellent' university – and excellence in her terms is defined in terms of 'places like Princeton, Oxford or Berkeley, Harvard, places like that'. Ralph Foxwell (Nortown Grammar) speaks of the need to be 'known' within his multina-tional organization:

I'd like to go abroad, because this organization is totally big in global organization . . . and if you're going to make a career in the organiza-tion you can't do it in one place. New York is the centre, so you've got to go to New York at some stage. Because who is ever going to know who you are if you've never been to New York!

Another dimension of the 'escalator effect' of the south-east is the extent to which the upwardly mobile subsequently leave the area. It is too early to say whether this will be the case for our respondents. Some were reluctant to go back 'north':

I don't get home to Nortown very often it has to be said. My mother is still in Nortown but I am not particularly fond of the place. I do like living in London, near London.

(Neil Gresham, Milltown Grammar)

Two female respondents, however, felt that they would be unlikely to remain in London, particularly when they 'settled down'.

> I'm going back up north. I'm not staying in London forever. It's on the cards for maybe next year or the year after . . . I do want kids, I want lots of kids, and I don't want to bring them up in London.
>
> (Nadia Healey, Cherry Tree)

> I see myself living in the south, but I'm an expatriate northerner. I'm a northerner through and through, and I'll go back home one day. I'll never settle in London. Not fully . . . But, I'm sort of living out my youth in London and that's enjoyable. But I would never bring children up here, if I had children.
>
> (Samantha Waters, Milltown High)

In the final sections of this chapter, we examine the future prospects of our respondents in relation to 'settling down', and consider the impact of this and their experiences of their own careers on their plans for their children.

Educational careers and family aspirations

Through both their schooling and their higher education we have found that women have performed as well as, if not better than, men. As we discussed in Chapter 9, their educational successes were not always reflected in equivalent earnings, except for those who went from elite universities into high-status occupations. However, we cannot presume that even these women will maintain their position in the future.

As we discussed earlier, a significant number of our respondents were uncertain about their future career directions. For many women, and for very few men, an added issue continues to be whether and when children arrive. Acker (1978: 123; cited in Spender 1981) points out that men can plan but women can only make contingency plans:

> In a sense they plan to do everything – job, housework, children, leisure, community involvement . . . women cannot really plan for the future given that her life in the decades ahead will be largely determined by a man she has not yet met, and children she has not yet had.

As we discussed in Chapter 9, some careers enable women to meet the contingencies of marriage, moves and children better than others, and we need to investigate the extent to which our women in 'non-traditional' and managerial positions are able to sustain their socio-economic status in future research.

Some might argue that just as middle-class careers are being redefined, so too are women's domestic careers. In terms of current domestic status, the

Table 10.1 Domestic arrangements

	No.	%
Married or living with a partner	101	30.6
Sharing with others	98	29.7
Living with parents	60	18.2
Living on their own	39	11.8
Other	9	2.7
Halls of residence	2	0.6
Combinations of the above	21	6.4
Total	330	100.0

largest group was living with a partner, but many were still living at home or sharing with others (see Table 10.1). In terms of marital status, the vast majority (over 90 per cent) were single. Twenty-nine (8 per cent) were married and two were divorced or separated. The overwhelming majority had not had children yet either. Only 19 respondents had children, of ages between a few months and six years.

Wilkinson and Mulgan's (1995) survey of young adults found that women are now less willing to raise children than men. However, this trend is not evident in our data. Domestic aspirations feature more prominently in our women respondents' accounts of what they will be doing in the future. After five and ten years, 52 respondents included 'starting a family' or 'marriage', but only three of these were male. For 21 of the 52 respondents, this was the principal descriptor of what they would be doing. The role our male respondents cast for themselves was traditional in its conception of being the 'breadwinner' even when they cited domestic aspirations:

A house and family on its way.

Earning a lot for a loving close family.

Building a secure home for my family.

The majority of the women in this sub-sample mentioned work futures as well as a family, although these were usually vague, e.g.

I imagine I will be working locally or part-time, whilst caring for a family.

At home with a family and teaching/counselling part-time.

Bringing up a family with part time work in a legal field.

Although these women were not anticipating giving up work entirely, they clearly saw themselves as having primary child care responsibilities. Work or studying were usually seen as secondary to this role:

I'd love to have a family, stay off work for a few years, and then go back to a really good job. I'm still looking for that. I don't want to be one of those mums who go straight back to work after their children and get someone else to look after them. I think that's the start of a lot of our problems, the children are not getting brought up right because their parents are not spending enough time with them. I'd like to do something, maybe an MSc, while I'm out of the workforce. That would do me! That would keep my mind ticking over, because when you're looking after kids you're not in touch with anybody when you're at home.

(Catherine Brunning, Rowton)

In ten years' time I'd hope to be a more general manager, perhaps just below director's level . . . What would alter the scenario would be if I had children. But probably I won't, probably I'll leave it ten years. If I had children, I'd want enough experience under my belt to be a consultant and be able to pick and choose what I do and look after my children and take on projects when I want to take them on.

(Natalie Jackman, Highgrove County)

All I've ever wanted was a family, but because of my upbringing I want to do the best I can now while I'm doing it. I'll go as high as I can and do as well as I can but at the end of the day it's not my goal. My goal is to have a family.

(Vanessa Heath, Vicarage Road)

Some women spoke to us of the difficulties that they would have with their colleagues and employers, e.g.

Particularly in a firm like this, which is mostly male partners. I don't think they've really come to terms with the idea that women are becoming solicitors and partners and they also have children. There was a lady who was a salaried partner and she's just had a child last October. She's come back part-time and now she's having another one and I know that my boss next door thinks it's a great inconvenience that Anna's had to go away and have another baby, just as she'd come back part-time and it was working so well. Yes, there are so many people in the law that think: 'Gosh, what an inconvenience.'

(Kristin Garrett, Milltown High)

And those traditional female occupations of teaching and nursing enabled them to consider re-entry or a sideways move at a later date:

I'd like to start a family within the next five years and I'll have teaching to come back to when I want to.

(Sadie Wiggin, Dame Margaret's)

In real terms, lecturing is a nice job for a married lady solicitor who has had a family. It's quite cushy.

(Kristin Garrett, Milltown High)

As a child I used to have a picture of myself in my sharp city suit and my briefcase, stalking along the street being terribly glamorous and high powered. And now, I do the job and it's a job that I feel that I can be proud of and that I do well, and it gives me a reasonable salary. But I've no urge to be managing director of ICI or anything like that anymore. I don't have those career ambitions. My ambitions are far more focused on my personal life than my work life . . . I have thought quite frequently about being a primary school teacher. It's something I think I would be good at and maybe enjoy a lot more than this type of job. But now I think it's probably not going to happen; or if it is going to happen maybe it will happen when I'm about 40, but not now. Realistically, I'll probably stay here for another two years. I hope to get married, hopefully, next year and I want to have children by the time I'm 30, so that's only another three years away. When I have children I'll probably stop working for a short period, but I'd always like to work part-time I think.

(Carol Joyce, Dame Margaret's)

Only four female respondents planned to combine family and 'upward' work aspirations:

Having children and be at the peak of my careeer maybe not in UK.

Working as a prosecution lawyer and a full time mother.

Financially secure, own practice, have family.

Running my own gallery, married with children.

Only two male respondents, when interviewed, discussed the impact of family on work career, and in one case the solution to the conflicting demands was to seek the 'comfort zone' through promotion:

I've come to the conclusion over the last year or two that certainly in Nissan – it's a very rewarding job, and I enjoy it a lot and it's very demanding – it's very demanding in terms of the work itself, and the hours you have to put in occasionally. Which is fine now, but I cannot see myself doing it when I'm married with a couple of kids – I won't want to do it, I'd refuse to spend that kind of time. It's great money that I'm going to be spending as compensation for the fact that I'm at work all the time. So what I think from that is to be promoted up to what I perceive as more of a comfort zone where the rewards outweigh the demands. And they are under a bit more pressure when they're there but they spend a lot less time at work, the managers.

(Christopher Scott, Rowton)

Educational futures of their children

When our respondents have reflected back on their careers, it has been clear that even those who appear 'successful' in terms of educational attainments and occupational destination can be marked by disappointment and uncertainty. As we have seen, even high academic achievement does not generate loyalty to a particular form of schooling, and many of those who were detached or estranged from their schools were quite insistent that they would not send any children of theirs to such an institution even when they themselves would have appeared to an outsider to have gained attainment benefits.

When asked in interview to speculate about the sorts of secondary schools they would send their own children to, just over half (54 per cent) of the ex-private school pupils were committed to using the private sector and 17 per cent said that they expected to use schools in the state sector. Many of those who were reluctant to send their own children to private schools focused on the problems of single-sex education rather than finance, social exclusivity or academic pressure. Many felt that their decision would depend on the particular character of the child. As Patrick Gourlay said of the thought of sending a son to Bankside College:

> If I thought a child of mine would get through it then yes I would send them there because I think you come out a far better educated and a far stronger person than when you went in. If you're not then you come out just crushed, you're a crushed person.

The idea of needing to be 'strong' to flourish in private schools is also evident in Keiran Warwick's (Nortown Grammar) comments:

> It's very difficult. I've thought about this. I've talked about it a lot with my girlfriend and it's very difficult. I guess it depends on how they turn out. If they're really rebellious, like I was, I think they would be better off in a public school. If they were the sort of children who can work and behave themselves, then I may as well send them to a state school.

However, many of the remaining 30 per cent who thought they might use either sector would only even contemplate a state school if it were selective and/or single-sex. Even when they supported the idea of state education in principle, they felt that the reality would make them more likely to use the private sector. Malcolm Jameson's (Nortown Grammar) response is typical of many:

> God, if there was a decent comprehensive school where we were living, fine. I've got no problems at all with sending a child to a state school. But obviously, as with most people I think, I want my child to achieve the best they can and be as happy as they can and if it looks as if

they're going to be better taught, have better facilities and so on at private school and money wasn't a problem, then I'd certainly send them to one.

Of those who were themselves schooled in the state sector, over 70 per cent expected to use the state sector, only 15 per cent anticipated using the private sector and 15 per cent thought they might use either. However, none of them was prepared to contemplate using just *any* state school and many said they would, if necessary, relocate to areas with grammar schools or comprehensive schools with strong academic records. Chloe Carter's (Vicarage Road) response reflects a common belief that principles can only prevail where the conditions allow:

I've always said 'yes I'd send them to a state school' and I'll pretty much to stick to that. However, I know it might change when you have children if you're in a situation and really if you were in an area where the state school's meant to be really bad. You don't know how you'd find that, maybe I would think 'well my children come first, I must put them in a private school'.

In the next chapter we explore how contemporary developments in education policy relate to the anxieties and dilemmas of middle-class parents as they attempt to ensure that their own children are destined for success.

Note

1 Because of the high level of mobility of our respondents, many were contacted and approached through their parents and some chose not to divulge current addresses to us. Some respondents are still in different forms of training, and some had moved between the questionnaire survey and subsequent interview, making it difficult to assign place of residence.

⟨11⟩ Including the middle class

Throughout this book, we have illustrated the complexity of the processes through which educational promise is or is not translated into educational and occupational 'success'. It is true that young people 'disproportionately from poor backgrounds in deprived areas', and with little educational success, take routes into adult life that are 'confused and lacking in clear goals and transition points'. By comparison, for those 'who do best at school . . . the achievement of high status qualifications and entry into the places they lead to, provide a clear goal and what can be seen as a "rite of passage"' (Social Exclusion Unit 1999: 8). Although almost all our respondents did well at school, and most came from middle-class homes, their progress was more vulnerable to interruption and diversion than the image of a rite of passage suggests. But as described in Chapters 4 and 6, almost all had followed the 'prime trajectory' that runs through A-levels and higher education into 'middle-class' employment, and almost none had even considered doing anything else. Although few had had specific 'futures' in mind when first interviewed early in their secondary schooling, most already had identities as successful learners and came from homes where firm causal connections were made between doing well at school and good prospects later. As we have described, the majority had also gone to schools where extended full-time education was so largely taken for granted that the few 'nonconformists' identified in Chapter 7 had resisted considerable pressures from family, school and peers in choosing otherwise. But these were exceptions.

As young adults, the fact that most were successful by comparison with a representative sample of their contemporaries drew most of our attention, in typical sociological fashion, to relative chances.

Any general conclusion that those who had gone to fee-paying schools were 'getting on' further or faster has to be qualified by differences within types of schooling, and by the many instances of unexpected success and failure. Nevertheless, despite ministerial insistence that standards, not structures, are what matter, we have reported some structural advantages from a system of secondary education still deeply divided on traditional lines between public and private provision, and between selective and non-selective schools. It focused our attention on the significance of these divisions for preserving social status, and for limiting competition from social and educational 'outsiders' for the more desirable credentials. As noted in the opening chapter, research in this area has been skewed by a preoccupation with elite recruitment. The much larger claim that private schooling has provided 'the main means of transferring economic status, social position and influence from generation to generation' (Labour Party 1980: 10) ignores the high proportions of 'established' middle-class families, and of 'incomers', who did not choose it. But it was more significant for our research that in so far as private schooling has been part of 'a self-reinforcing virtuous circle' for those families who could afford it (Hutton 1995: 213), or were able to take advantage of assisted places, the benefits attributed to it have changed markedly since the times when it was at least as much a confirmation of status as an acquisition of new cultural capital.

The obvious change has been the much closer association of those benefits with academic success. This is why the claim can be made that the private sector has changed in a few decades from 'a disparate and vulnerable collection of institutions' not generally noted for 'scholarship' into 'a fairly unified structure of four hundred private meritocratic academies' (Adonis and Pollard 1998: 43–5). The conclusion drawn from that description is that England has moved towards a 'class meritocracy' – a divided system that is both meritocratic and socially exclusive. It is a meritocracy in so far as private schooling 'deserves' its prominence in class recruitment by its high share of the best A-level results and of entry to the 'best' universities. It is class-based because access to private schooling is largely determined by birth.

This conclusion corresponds with Halsey's (1995) view that, while the labour market has become more meritocratic, the education market may have become less meritocratic as middle-class families have recognized the increasing importance of qualifications and worked to improve their children's relative chances of getting 'the best' of them. Saunders (1996, 1997) accepted the first proposition but not the second. His own optimistic conclusion was that as employment prospects have become more closely linked to qualifications and as these have become available in schools of all kinds, so social class and type of schooling matters much less than its duration and outcomes. Outside a few esoteric elites, he claimed, the meritocratic equation 'ability + effort = success' now very largely applies. That equation is inherently untestable because ability is measured and accredited according to criteria shaped in favour of the already advantaged (Goldthorpe 1997). Indeed, Saunders's reanalysis of National Child Development Study data (from a cohort some 12 years older than our respondents) led him to concede that more than a third of the middle-class entrants to middle-class occupations had not 'deserved' to do so by ability, a proportion substantially greater than from other social classes (Saunders 1996: 69–70).

Our privately schooled informants were certainly not 'undeserving' of their educational success, as they were all deemed to be academically able. But their generally better A-level performance did not entirely explain why they had been twice as likely to go to 'elite' universities, were significantly more likely to have taken the most marketable traditional-academic and traditional-vocational degree courses and were more likely to be already in higher-level professional and managerial jobs and in the higher-earning income band. These findings appear to support claims that the socially advantaged remain disproportionately successful at gaining access to institutions capable of reinforcing their advantages, and that 'the old structures by which pathways to occupational achievement were established in the past are still quite firmly in place' (Bynner *et al.* 1997: 50–1).

This book has largely been about the 'old structures' of private and elective schooling. And our focus on middle-class education and employment partly reflects changes in the nature of British society over the past 40 years, and partly a shift in educational research away from a longstanding preoccupation with 'researching down' (Walford 1994). Most of all, it recognizes that educational inequalities need to be understood relationally.

With education having become an increasingly significant positional good, middle-class choice strategies have implications for others which may be even more significant than in the past. Ball *et al.* (1996) argued that 'skilful and resourceful' middle-class parents were always able to 'work the system' to their advantage and that the actions of families are as important as those of schools in maintaining social class divisions and inequalities. While their study focused on the 'reinforcement' of such tendencies by recent government promotion of parental choice, and the creation of another set of class-related processes, our research suggests that 'playing the market' was already well established in the early 1980s and that some consequent advantages were evident a decade or so later. We therefore conclude with comments on New Labour approaches to educational opportunity, several of which seem to us to reflect the particular account taken of middle-class views and priorities (McCaig 2000).

Some policy pronouncements have displayed a notable lack of 'relational' thinking, those on school choice appearing at times to echo Mrs Thatcher's notorious dictum that there is 'no such thing as society, only individuals and families'. Yet in a stratified society, apparently equitable arrangements for choosing schools can effectively enable those with the material and cultural resources to make the best choices to deny those choices to others. As a former 'Old Labour' minister put it, school choice gives freedom to middle-class parents 'to talk their way into unfair advantage' (Roy Hattersley, *Observer*, 15 January 1995). And we have described how that choice is implicated in the reproduction of the English middle class and its various 'old' and 'new' fractions. Relational thinking is clearly evident in Giddens' (1998) observation that 'social exclusion' is a dual process, operating at the 'top' as well as the 'bottom' of society. Traditionally, upper- and upper middle-class families in England have 'self-excluded' themselves from mainstream educational provision by their use of elite private schooling, although the rapid growth of the middle class since the 1950s has not led to a similar growth in the size of that sector of education and we questioned the existence of a distinctive closed 'private schooling' class (Burchardt *et al.* 1999). Thus we described how parts of the middle class have made increasing use of the private sector, using either their own or the state's resources to do so, but also noted how middle-class families have successfully 'colonized' parts of the public sector. This partly explains how some comprehensives have become relatively safe alternatives to fee-paying and other forms of selective secondary education, and this has led to the emergence in some schools – especially those in control of their own admissions and seeking to attract a particular middle-class clientele – of 'reinvented traditionalism' (Halpin *et al.* 1997).

On the face of it, school type no longer appears to have that direct relationship to social reproduction that was manifest in Victorian England and later. Most of the young people in our study had successful educational careers in a variety of public and private, selective and non-selective contexts. In such conventional terms as entry to higher education, the vast majority of a cohort identified as 'destined for success' at age 11 could be regarded as having broadly realized their academic potential, and so to have 'deserved' good occupational prospects. However, the closer examination we have attempted makes it clear that certain choices still bring a significantly greater chance of conventionally 'successful' careers than others, particularly when the competition is for the 'glittering prizes' associated with elite universities and elite occupations. These choices included academically 'safe' comprehensives, but they were most conspicuous in relation to private schooling. Middle-class preoccupations with making the 'right' choice of school were explored in Chapter 3, and from a time just prior to a substantial 'empowerment' of (some) consumers within the state system.

In broad terms, those of our respondents who had gone to academically selective private schools tended to attain higher levels of academic success than their peers from comprehensive schools. Although their academic success generally seems to have depended more on educational inheritance than the type of school attended, those with little educational capital in terms of parental education appear to have gained most from attending private schools provided they stayed on into the sixth form. This might seem to support a very familiar argument for academic selection, that it carries clever children from poor homes into an environment of high aspirations that counteracts the unsupportive influences of neighbourhood and peers. The Labour government's prompt dismantling of the traditional escape route provided by assisted places has prompted efforts to replace them through appeals for private funds, by individual schools like Manchester Grammar School (with a target of £10 million), by the Girls' Day Schools Trust (with a target of £70 million) and by several charities, exemplified by the Sutton Trust. That body's founder has argued for 'access by ability' to the best private schools, thereby changing their social class base and breaking the link between 'wealth and opportunity' (Lampl 1999). In its most recent analysis of the damage caused by a two-nation school system in which the gap between the privileged and unprivileged is widening, 'open access' is described significantly as a 'third way approach' (Sutton Trust 2001: 3). This may be a deliberate reference to the part of Third Way theory that insists on replacing 'egalitarianism at all costs' with a 'dynamic life chances approach' that gives clear priority to equality of opportunity over past (and futile) efforts to equalize outcomes. From that perspective, even greater inequalities of outcome are justified if they arise from merit, that combination of ability and effort mentioned earlier (Giddens 2000: 86).

Focusing on escape routes from 'second-best' state provision seems to us to display insufficiently relational thinking. School-type or school-sector effects on academic performance, in so far as the evidence supports them, are partly explained by the impact of selection itself upon the composition of comprehensive schools, and particularly on their capacity to provide for academically able students. That many 'comprehensive' schools have highly unbalanced intakes is well documented. There may have been by the 1990s far more academically able children in comprehensive schools than 20 years earlier, but they were so unevenly distributed that only half the schools covered had the 15 per cent or more of such children commonly regarded as necessary to support an academic ethos (Benn and Chitty 1996: 179). Put another way, higher socio-economic status children were most likely to attend the least comprehensive of comprehensive schools (Kerckhoff *et al.* 1996: 268). As we described in Chapter 5, many of our comprehensive school respondents had been supported in their aspirations by like-minded peers and thereby helped to create their own academically supportive environment. This is why benefits attributed to selection have to be balanced against the potential costs to academically able students who remain in comprehensive schools denied a 'critical mass' of 'more engaged, broadly "pro-school" children to start with' (Maden 2001: 336).

Giddens' (1998) own argument about social exclusion as a dual and relational process is directly relevant here. As Young (1999) points out, exclusion 'at the top' and 'at the bottom' are interdependent in quite specific ways. For example, families with high enough incomes to afford alternatives avoid the state secondary schools in many inner London boroughs precisely because many of the students in such schools are from families who would on any criteria be classified as being among the excluded 'at the bottom'. The falling quality of public services in the inner cities is thus partly an outcome of the withdrawal of support by growing numbers of relatively better off people. In boroughs where better off families continue to use public secondary schools, they have often used other mechanisms of 'exclusion at the top', such as moving house into the catchment of the best state schools, using position and influence to avoid less successful schools or pressing hard for the creation of academic 'schools within schools' through strong and early streaming. Recent school choice policies have facilitated this strategic withdrawal of middle-class families from disadvantaged schools (Whitty *et al.* 1998), making it even more difficult for these schools to succeed.

From a consequent interest in providing escape routes, it might be concluded from our study that more effectively designed and targeted assisted places would indeed provide a way of challenging the middle-class monopoly of those educational resources most likely to secure a place in the middle classes of the next generation. Yet the traditional practice of sponsoring 'meritorious' working-class children into middle-class schools, both private and public, has served to legitimate the wider system without threatening middle-class interests. Advocacy of a wholesale return to academic selection in the public sector, which has revived in recent years, raises the old objections to social bias in the identification of 'ability' and to its identification 'prematurely' (Freeman 1998). More significantly, it would reinforce the assumption – made by many parents in the original study of the Assisted Places Scheme – that comprehensive schools as such perform less well, and so provide fewer opportunities, than selective schools. Recent research suggests that the evidence for the latter's 'superiority' is at best inconclusive (Crook *et al.* 1999), or diminishes into insignificance when the social background and prior attainment of their intakes is taken adequately into account (Gorard 2000).

No clear-cut conclusions can be drawn from our own study about appropriate and fair provision for academically able children. Taken together, our questionnaire and interview data indicate that different kinds of schools exert different kinds of pressure for high achievement. It is a common assumption that such children suffer in comprehensive schools by being in a small minority. And it was indeed at these schools that more of our respondents had worried about being thought 'too clever'. But the ease with which schoolwork had been balanced with outside interests seemed to depend a great deal on finding a peer group with similar inclinations and aspirations. While this could not be taken for granted, tolerance of a greater range of subcultures had avoided those tensions experienced by some respondents from highly selective schools ill-at-ease with features of the expressive order, notably the emphasis on team sports and the insistence on loyalty to the school at the expense of more local (neighbourhood) attachments.

In general, as we reported in Chapter 5, academically selective schools appeared, predictably, to be more effective at providing consistent alignment between students, peer groups and school interests. Travelling time, homework and the schools' perceived exclusiveness made it difficult for respondents to maintain an 'external' social life, thus focusing peer group activity within a school ambit and in the company of academically able and often ambitious students like themselves. Even so, competition for conspicuous academic success could be intense, even though boys in particular had often found it socially unacceptable to engage too visibly in academic work. Even in the most academically oriented and competitive girls' selective schools this seemed to have been less of a worry, and the complex relationship between school ethos, peer group influences and gender identification goes some way towards explaining the greater polarization of boys' attainments that we reported in Chapter 4. For some students of both sexes, the mode of sponsorship had created additional pressures. Some of the full-fee payers were keenly aware of the sacrifices their parents had made to send them to these schools, and consequently felt guilty when they had not fulfilled their expectations. Some assisted place holders with lower levels of educational inheritance reported both struggling with the work and feeling 'out of place'. The less totalizing ethos of comprehensive schools could provide a less constrained environment, but could also detract from that 'pull' towards academic success that is often used to explain working-class underachievement.

The contrasting individual experiences of the 'same' school that we have described highlight the importance of home background, and of particular influences on the course of school careers. Given the significant differences between the performance of individual schools in all sectors, and in the responses of different students to particular types of school, it is important to explore what features enable schools to work successfully with academically able students from widely differing family backgrounds. It will also be important to identify schools that are particularly successful in sponsoring the kinds of talent that tend to be overlooked in conventional schemes of academic selection such as the Assisted Places Scheme. This is the approach taken in the Excellence in Cities initiative, which makes it unfortunate that government promotion of partnerships between private and state schools seems to take it for granted that all the useful learning will be by state schools. The logic of seeing social exclusion as a dual process is that any programme for social inclusion must also be a dual process. Strategies are needed to include 'the top' as well as 'the bottom' of society within the mainstream of public provision. The government's agenda has appeared to be focused largely on mapping 'exclusion at the bottom' (Young 1999), although the specialist schools programme has been interpreted as deliberately designed to 'achieve two antagonistic goals: encouraging the middle classes to use the state sector while simultaneously raising levels of provision in Britain's worst-off communities' (Penlington 2001: 9). This may also be reflected in Excellence in Cities. Whatever its intentions, and they were certainly not clear at the time of its launch, that initiative has often been claimed as one of the success stories of New Labour education policy in retaining middle-class children in inner-city state schools while also raising achievement among working-class groups (Morris 2002). Even so, getting the balance right between the potentially positive effects of 'critical mass' and the dangers of middle-class 'colonization' of schools and their curricula at the expense of working-class families will be difficult. Indeed, difficulties of this sort have already been reported in connection with the 'Gifted and Talented' strand of the initiative (Lucey and Reay 2002). Nevertheless, Excellence in Cities may herald the beginnings of a dual strategy of social inclusion, which addresses middle-class concerns while pursuing a more radical agenda to challenge the notion that academic ability is only to be found among middle-class children. If so, it could help to break the enduring link in English education between pursuing excellence and perpetuating privilege. But that will only happen if such policies are articulated with others that address those wider economic and cultural inequalities which influence education. Differential access to educational provision is associated not only with enduring differences between social classes but also, as this book has shown, differences within the middle class itself.

Appendix A: Gazeteer of schools mentioned in the text (by pseudonym)

Archbishop Ambrose Grammar School A maintained grammar school for boys. It had about 850 pupils aged 11–18. Many of its sixth-formers proceeded into higher education, including a considerable number going up to Oxbridge. Its head was one of the few state school members of the Headmasters' Conference (HMC).

Bankside College A traditional boys' public school, it had over 600 pupils, mainly boarders. Girls were formerly admitted into the sixth form but at the time of the study it had recently opened its doors to girls at 13. Over 80 per cent of its pupils moved into the sixth form, with over 50 per cent entering university.

Cathedral College A leading public school which took day boys and boarders. There were 700 pupils in the school. A small number of girls were admitted into the sixth form. It had a small preparatory school that prepared boys for the Common Entrance examination. Pupils entered the college at 13. The school offered a small number of assisted places and a large number of its own scholarships.

Cherry Tree Comprehensive School A coeducational school of over 1500 pupils. Based on two former secondary modern schools, it was well supported by local parents. Some 60 per cent of fifth-year pupils entered its sixth form. Seventy-five per cent of A-level leavers went on to higher or further education.

Dame Margaret's High School An independent school for girls with about 550 pupils on roll, aged 11–18. It also had a small preparatory school, taking girls aged 7–11. It awarded its own bursaries in the senior school in addition to the assisted places available.

Frampton Comprehensive School   A mixed school with 800 pupils aged 11–18, it was formerly a secondary modern school. That history, and the predominantly working-class catchment area it served, were reflected in its relatively small sixth form.

Highgrove County School for Girls   This maintained grammar school had nearly 1000 pupils. They were selected by a borough-wide entrance examination conducted by the LEA, supplemented by primary school reports. It had a strong sixth form with a high proportion of its leavers moving into further and higher education.

Milltown Grammar School for Boys   A former direct-grant school, it was a fully independent day school attended by 650 boys. It shared a site with the girls' division and both were administered by the same foundation. Ninety per cent of its pupils stayed on to the sixth form, and over 60 per cent of its A-level leavers went on to university.

Milltown High School for Girls   The girls' equivalent of Milltown Grammar, it had 500 pupils aged 11–18 on roll. There was a junior division attached to the school for girls aged 9–11. A strong sixth form shared some facilities with the boys' school. Many of the A-level leavers moved into further or higher education.

Moorside Comprehensive School   A mixed school with 1500 pupils, this school was organized on traditional lines and it had a good reputation locally. It had developed a large sixth form, which helped to convince parents that it would cater for academically able pupils.

Nortown Grammar School   Formerly a direct-grant school, this large day school for boys had a formidable academic reputation. Over three-quarters of its leavers went on to university, including a large number to Oxbridge. From its own resources it was able to offer scholarships to many of its meritorious pupils.

Nortown High School   A girls' independent school with 500 pupils aged 11–18. A former direct-grant school, it had retained that earlier tradition by its performance in public examinations and by the large proportion of its A-level leavers entering higher education.

Parkside Girls' School   This girls' comprehensive school had 950 pupils aged 11–16, and it was formerly a maintained grammar school. It had strong support from those parents who believed that a single-sex education had significant academic benefits for girls but who wished their daughters to be educated in a state school.

Rowton Comprehensive School   Formed by the amalgamation of two secondary modern schools, this mixed comprehensive had 1600 pupils aged 11–18. There were nearly 150 pupils in the sixth form. Its socially mixed catchment area included council estates and more affluent middle-class suburbs.

St Hilda's Girls' School   An independent day school for approximately 600 pupils, its catchment area covered the Riverside area and beyond. Most of its pupils stayed on for A-levels and it had an impressive pass rate in those examinations. About 90 per cent of its leavers went on to higher education. Founders' scholarships were available for academically meritorious pupils.

Shirebrook School   This mixed comprehensive school of 1000 pupils aged 13–18 drew pupils from a socially mixed, mainly rural catchment area. However, it had attracted numbers of educationally ambitious parents, satisfied that its academic performance at O- and A-levels and its success in providing university entrants met their needs.

Vicarage Road Comprehensive School   A mixed school with approximately 950 pupils aged 11–16. It was a former secondary modern school and had had to work hard to throw off that image locally. However, with buildings refurbished and a new headteacher, it had been recruiting well in the borough and in the adjacent LEA.

Weston School   A small independent boys' school in a rural location, it was predominantly a boarding school but admitted some day pupils. Girls had recently been admitted to its sixth form. Entry was at 13 and there were about 300 pupils in the main school.

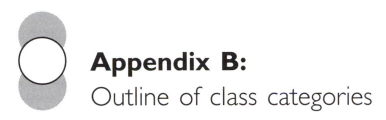

Appendix B:
Outline of class categories

We outline here the definitions of social classes based on occupation in the Standard Occupational Classification system developed by the Office of Population Censuses and Surveys (OPCS 1991).

I: Professional etc.   These include the following kinds of employment: general administrators at national government level; engineering professions; health professionals (e.g. medical/dental practitioners); university teachers; legal professionals; accountants; architects; solicitors etc.

II: Managerial and technical.   These include the following kinds of employment: general managers of large companies and organizations; local government officers; protective service officers (e.g. senior police, prison officers); school and FE teachers; town planners; nurses etc.

III NM: Skilled (non-manual).   These include: clerks, cashiers; sales personnel; draughtpersons; secretaries; those working in food preparation etc.

III M: Skilled (manual).   These include: skilled workers in the construction trades; those working in electrical and vehicle trades; textile, craft and related occupations; laboratory technicians etc.

IV: Partly skilled.   These include: machine setters and operators; security and protective service occupations (e.g. junior policy officers, security guards); waiters and bar staff etc.

V: Unskilled.   These include: unskilled workers in construction; mining; manufacturing; occupations in transport and labouring.

 References

Acker, S. (1978) Sex differences in graduate student ambition. Unpublished PhD, University of Bristol.

Adnett, N. and Davies, P. (2000) Competition and curriculum diversity in local schooling markets: theory and evidence, *Journal of Education Policy*, 15: 157–67.

Adonis, A. and Pollard, S. (1998) *A Class Act: The Myth of Britain's Classless Society*. London: Penguin Books.

Aggleton, P. (1987) *Rebels without a Cause?* Lewes: Falmer Press.

Ainley, P. (1994) *Degrees of Difference: Higher Education in the 1990s*. London: Lawrence and Wishart.

Anisef, A., Turrittin, A. and Zeng, L. (1999) Social and geographical mobility twenty years after high school, in W. Heinz (ed.) *From Education to Work: Cross-national Perspectives*. Cambridge: Cambridge University Press.

Anon (1861) Middle class education in England: past and present. Extract from *Cornhill* magazine, July.

Arnold, M. (1892) *A French Eton, or Middle Class Education and the State*. London: Macmillan.

Arnot, M., David, M. and Weiner, G. (1999) *Closing the Gender Gap: Post-war Educational and Social Change*. Cambridge: Polity Press.

Ball, S. (1981) *Beachside Comprehensive: A Case-study of Secondary Schooling*. Cambridge: Cambridge University Press.

Ball, S. (1994) *Education Reform: A Critical and Post-structural Approach*. Buckingham: Open University Press.

Ball, S. and Gewirtz, S. (1997) Girls in the education market: choice, competition and complexity, *Gender and Education*, 9: 207–22.

Ball, S., Bowe, R. and Gewirtz, S. (1996) School choice, social class and distinction: the realisation of social advantage in education, *Journal of Education Policy*, 11(1): 89–112.

Ball, S., Macrae, S. and Maguire, M. (1999) Young lives, diverse choices and imagined futures in an education and training market, *International Journal of Inclusive Education*, 3(3): 195–224.

Ball, S., Maguire, M. and Macrae, S. (2000) *Choice, Pathways and Transitions Post 16: New Youth, New Economies in the Global City*. London: Routledge/Falmer.

Ball, S., Davies, J., David, M. and Reay, D. (2002) 'Classification' and 'judgement': social class and the 'cognitive structures' of choice of higher education, *British Journal of Sociology of Education*, 23(1): 51–72.

Banks, M., Bates, I., Breakwell, G. *et al.* (1992) *Careers and Identities*. Buckingham: Open University Press.

Benn, C. and Chitty, C. (1996) *Thirty Years On: Is Comprehensive Education Alive and Well, or Struggling to Survive?* London: David Fulton.

Berghoff, H. (1990) Public schools and the decline of the British economy 1870–1914, *Past and Present*, 129: 148–67.

Bernstein, B. (1971) *Class, Codes and Control, Volume 1. Theoretical Studies Towards a Sociology of Language*. London: Routledge and Kegan Paul.

Bernstein, B. (1977) *Class, Codes and Control, Volume 3*, 2nd edn. London: Routledge and Kegan Paul.

Bernstein, B. (1990) *The Structuring of Pedagogic Discourse: Class, Codes and Control, Volume 4*. London: Routledge.

Bernstein, B. (1996) *Pedagogy, Symbolic Control and Identity: Theory, Research, Critique*. London: Taylor & Francis.

Bernstein, B. (1999) Official knowledge and pedagogic identities, in F. Christie (ed.) *Pedagogy and the Shaping of Consciousness*. London and New York: Cassell.

Biggart, A. and Furlong, A. (1996) Educating 'discouraged' workers: cultural diversity in the upper secondary school, *British Journal of Sociology of Education*, 17(3): 253–66.

Blackburn, R. and Jarman, J. (1993) Changing inequalities in access to British universities, *Oxford Review of Education*, 19(2): 197–213.

Blackburn, R. and Marsh, C. (1991) Education and social class: revisiting the 1944 Education Act with fixed marginals, *British Journal of Sociology*, 42: 507–36.

Blair, T. (1999) Speech delivered 14 January, IPPR. www.number-10.gov.uk.

Boudon, R. (1974) *Education, Opportunity and Social Inequality*. New York: John Wiley.

Bourdieu, P. (1976) The school as a conservative force, in R. Dale, G. Esland and M. MacDonald (eds) *Schooling and Capitalism*. London: Routledge and Kegan Paul.

Bourdieu, P. (1984) *Distinction: A Social Critique of the Judgement of Taste*, trans. Richard Nice. London: Routledge.

Bourdieu, P. (1990) *The Logic of Practice*. Cambridge: Polity Press.

Bourdieu, P. (1998) *The State Nobility: Elite Schools in the Field of Power*. Cambridge: Polity Press.

Boys, C. J. and Kirkland, J. (1988) *Degrees of Success*. London: Jessica Kingsley.

Breen, R. and Goldthorpe, J. H. (1997) Explaining educational differences: towards a formal rational action theory, *Rationality and Society*, 9(3): 275–305.

Brown, P. (1995) Cultural capital and social exclusion: some observations on recent trends in education, employment and the labour market, *Work, Employment and Society*, 9: 29–51.

Brown, P. and Scase, R. (1994) *Higher Education and Corporate Realities: Class, Culture and the Decline of Graduate Careers*. London: UCL Press.

Burchardt, T., Hills, J. and Propper, C. (1999) *Private Welfare and Public Policy*. York: Joseph Rowntree Foundation.

Butler, T. and Savage, M. (eds) (1995) *Social Change and the Middle Classes*. London: UCL Press.

Bynner, J. (1999) New routes to employment: integration and exclusion, in W. Heinz (ed.) *From Education to Work: Cross-national Perspectives*. Cambridge: Cambridge University Press.

Bynner, J., Ferri, E. and Shepherd, P. (eds) (1997) *Twenty-something in the 1990s: Getting On, Getting By, and Getting Nowhere*. Aldershot: Ashgate.

Clarricoates, K. (1978) Dinosaurs in the classroom – a re-examination of some aspects of the 'hidden curriculum' in primary schools, *Women's Studies International Quarterly*, 1: 353–64.

Cobban, J. (1969) The direct-grant school, in C. Cox and A. Dyson (eds) *The Fight for Education*. London: Critical Quarterly Society.

Cockett, M. and Callaghan, J. (1996) Caught in the middle: transition at 16+, in R. Halsall and M. Cockett (eds) *Education and Training 14–19: Chaos or Coherence?* London: David Fulton.

Connell, R. (1989) Cool guys, swots and wimps: the interplay of masculinity and education, *Oxford Review of Education*, 15: 291–303.

Connell, R. (1996) *Masculinities*. Cambridge: Polity Press.

Connell, R., Ashenden, D., Kessler, S. and Dowsett, G. (1983) *Making the Difference: Schools, Families and Social Division*. London: Allen & Unwin.

Cookson, P. and Persell, C. (1985) English and American residential secondary schools: a comparative study of the reproduction of social elites, *Comparative Education Review*, 29(3): 283–98.

Corrigan, P. (1979) *Schooling the Smash Street Kids*. London: Macmillan.

Crompton, R. (1992) Where did all the bright girls go? Women's higher education and employment since 1964, in A. Abercrombie and A. Warde (eds) *Social Change in Contemporary Britain*. Cambridge: Polity Press.

Crompton, R. and Sanderson, K. (1990) *Gendered Jobs and Social Change*. London: Unwin Hyman.

Crook, S., Power, S. and Whitty, G. (1999) *The Grammar School Question: Review of Research on Comprehensive and Selective Education*. London: Institute of Education.

David, M., West, A. and Ribbens, J. (1994) *Mother's Intuition: Choosing Secondary Schools*. London: Falmer Press.

Davis, R. (1967) *The Grammar School*. Harmondsworth: Penguin.

Delamont, S. (1984) Debs, dollies, swots and weeds: classroom styles at St. Lukes', in G. Walford (ed.) *British Public Schools*. London: Falmer.

Delamont, S. (1989) *Knowledgeable Women*. London: Routledge.

Du Bois-Reymond, M. (1998) 'I don't want to commit myself yet': young people's life concepts, *Journal of Youth Studies*, 1(1): 63–79.

Dunleavy, P. (1980) The political implications of sectoral cleavages and the growth of state employment: part 2, cleavage structures and political alignment, *Political Studies*, 28: 527–49.

Duru-Bellat, M. (2000) Social inequalities in the French education system: the joint effect of individual and contextual factors, *Journal of Education Policy*, 15: 33–40.

Edwards, T. (1997) Educating leaders and training followers, in T. Edwards, C. Fitz-Gibbon, F. Hardman, R. Haywood and N. Meagher, *Separate but Equal? A-levels and GNVQs*. London: Routledge.

Edwards, T. and Whitty, G. (1997) Marketing quality: traditional and modern versions of educational excellence, in R. Glatter, P. Woods and C. Bagley (eds) *Choice and Diversity in Schooling*. London: Routledge.

Edwards, T., Fitz, J. and Whitty, G. (1989) *The State and Private Education: An Evaluation of the Assisted Places Scheme*. Basingstoke: Falmer Press.

Egerton, M. (1997) Occupational inheritance: the role of cultural capital and gender, *Work, Employment and Society*, 11: 263–82.

Epstein, D. (1996) Real boys don't work: underachievement, masculinity and the harassment of sissies. Paper presented to the ESRC Seminar Series 'Gender and Education: Are Boys now Underachieving?', Institute of Education, 15 November.

Epstein, D. (ed.) (1998) *Failing Boys*. Buckingham: Open University Press.

Epstein, D. and Johnson, R. (1998) *Schooling Sexualities*. Buckingham: Open University Press.

Erikson, R. and Goldthorpe, J. (1992) *The Constant Flux: A Study of Class Mobility in Industrial Societies*. Oxford: Clarendon Press.

Evans, K. and Furlong, A. (1996) Metaphors of youth transitions: niches, pathways, trajectories or navigations?, in J. Bynner, L. Chisholm and A. Furlong (eds) *Youth, Citizenship and Social Change*. Aldershot: Ashgate.

Fielding, T. (1995) Migration and middle-class formation in England and Wales, 1981–91, in T. Butler and M. Savage (eds) *Social Change and the Middle Classes*. London: UCL Press.

Fitch, J. G. (1865) *Royal Commission of Enquiry into the State of Middle Class Education*. London: Edward Stanford.

Ford, J. (1969) *Social Class and the Comprehensive School*. London: Routledge and Kegan Paul.

Fox, I. (1984) The demand for a public school education: a crisis of confidence in comprehensive schooling, in G. Walford (ed.) *British Public Schools: Policy and Practice*. Lewes: Falmer Press.

Freeman, J. (1998) *Educating the Very Able: Current International Research*. London: The Stationery Office.

Galland, O. and Oberti, M. (2000) Higher education students in contemporary France, *Journal of Education Policy*, 15(1): 105–16.

Giddens, A. (1984) *The Constitution of Society*. Cambridge: Polity Press.

Giddens, A. (1998) *The Third Way: The Renewal of Social Democracy*. Cambridge: Polity Press.

Giddens, A. (2000) *The Third Way and its Critics*. Cambridge: Polity Press.

Glennerster, H. (1995) *British Social Policy since 1945*. Oxford: Blackwell.

Glennerster, H. and Wilson, G. (1970) *Paying for Private Schools*. London: Allen Lane.

Goldthorpe, J. H. (1982) On the service class, its formation and future, in A. Giddens and G. Mackenzie (eds) *Social Class and the Division of Labour*. Cambridge: Cambridge University Press.

Goldthorpe, J. H. (1995) The service class revisited, in T. Butler and M. Savage (eds) *Social Change and the Middle Classes*. London: University College London Press.

Goldthorpe, J. H. (1997) Problems of meritocracy, in A. Halsey, H. Lauder, P. Brown and A. Wells (eds) *Education: Culture, Economy, Society*. Oxford: Oxford University Press.

Gorard, S. (1997) *School Choice in an Established Market*. Aldershot: Ashgate Press.

Gorard, S. (2000) Questioning the crisis account: a review of evidence for increasing polarisation in schools, *Educational Research*, 42: 309–21.

Gosden, P. (1976) *Education and the Second World War*. London: Methuen.

Graham, D. with Tytler, D. (1993) *A Lesson for Us All: The Making of the National Curriculum*. London: Routledge.

Green, A. (1990) *Education and State Formation*. London: Macmillan.

Halpin, D., Power, S. and Fitz, J. (1997) Opting into the past? Grant maintained schools and the reinvention of tradition, in R. Glatter, P. Woods and C. Bagley (eds) *Choice and Diversity in Schooling*. London: Routledge.

Halsey, A. (1995) *Change in British Society*, 4th edn. Oxford: Oxford University Press.

Halsey, A. and McCrum, N. (2000) The slow but certain arrival of equality at Oxford University, *Times Higher Education Supplement*, 17 November, 22.

Halsey, A., Health, A. and Ridge, J. (1980) *Origins and Destinations: Family, Class, and Education in Modern Britain*. Oxford: Clarendon Press.

Halsey, A., Heath, A. and Ridge, J. (1984) The political arithmetic of public schools, in G. Walford (ed.) *British Public Schools: Policy and Practice*. Lewes: Falmer Press.

Hanlon, G. (1998) Professionalism as enterprise: service class politics and the redefinition of professionalism, *Sociology*, 32(1): 43–63.

Harris, I. M. (1995) *Messages Men Hear: Constructing Masculinities*. London: Taylor & Francis.

Heath, A. and Cheung, S. (1996) Education and occupation in Britain, in W. Mueller and Y. Shavitt (eds) *Education and Entry to the Labour Market in Comparative Perspective*. Boulder, CO: Westview Press.

Heath, A. and Clifford, P. (1996) Class inequalities and educational reform in twentieth-century Britain, in D. Lee and B. Turner (eds) *Conflicts about Class: Debating Inequality in Late Industrialism*. London: Longman.

Heath, A. and Ridge, J. (1983) Schools, examinations and occupational attainment, in J. Purvis and M. Hales (eds) *Achievement and Inequality in Education*. London: Routledge.

Heath, A. and Savage, M. (1995) Political alignments within the middle-classes 1972–89, in T. Butler and M. Savage (eds) *Social Change and the Middle Classes*. London: University College.

Heath, A., Mills, C. and Roberts, J. (1992) Towards meritocracy? Recent evidence on an old problem, in C. Crouch and A. Heath (eds) *Social Research and Social Reform*. Oxford: Clarendon Press.

Heward, C. (1988) *Making a Man of Him: Parents and Their Sons' Education at an English Public School 1929–1950*. London: Routledge.

Heward, C. and Taylor, P. (1993) Effective and ineffective equal opportunities policies in higher education, *Critical Social Policy*, 37: 75–94.

Hirsch, D. (1997) Policies for school choice: what can Britain learn from abroad?, in R. Glatter, P. Woods and C. Bagley (eds) *Choice and Diversity in Schooling*. London: Routledge.

Hodkinson, P. and Sparkes, A. (1997) Careership: a sociological theory of career decision-making, *British Journal of Sociology of Education*, 18(1): 29–44.

Honey, J. (1977) *Tom Brown's Universe: The Development of the Victorian Public School*. London: Millington.

Hutber, P. (1976) *The Decline and Fall of the Middle Class and How It Can Fight Back*. London: Associated Business Programmes.

Hutton, W. (1995) *The State We're In*. London: Jonathan Cape.

ISIS (1994) *Annual Census*. London: Independent Schools Information Service.

Jackson, B. and Marsden, D. (1966) *Education and the Working-class*. Harmondsworth: Pelican Books.

Kalton, G. (1966) *The Public Schools: A Factual Survey*. London: Longman.

Kamm, J. (1971) *Indicative Past: A Hundred Years of the Girls' Public Day Schools Trust*. London: Allen & Unwin.

Kerckhoff, A. C., Fogelman, K., Crook, D. and Reeder, D. (1996) *Going Comprehensive in England and Wales: A Study of Uneven Change*. London: Woburn Press.

Kerckhoff, A., Fogelman, K. and Manilove, J. (1997) Staying ahead: the middle class and school reform in England and Wales, *Sociology of Education*, 70: 19–35.

Killeen, J., Turton, R., Diamond, W., Dosnon, O. and Wach, M. (1999) Education and the labour market: subjective aspects of human capital investment, *Journal of Education Policy*, 14: 99–116.

King, R. (1976) Bernstein's sociology of the school: some propositions tested, *British Journal of Sociology*, 27: 430–43.

King, R. (1981) Bernstein's sociology of the school: a further testing, *British Journal of Sociology*, 32: 259–65.

Labour Party (1980) *Private Schools: A Discussion Document*. London: Labour Party.

Lampl, P. (1999) Opening up elite education, *Prospect*, January: 52–5.

Lash, S. and Urry, J. (1987) *The End of Organized Capitalism*. Cambridge: Polity Press.

Lawson, J. and Silver, H. (1973) *A Social History of Education in England*. London: Methuen.

Leonard, D. (1996) The debate around co-education, in S. Kemal, D. Leonard, M. Pringle and S. Sadeque (eds) *Targeting Underachievement: Boys or Girls?* London: Institute of Education/CREG.

Lewis, R. and Maude, A. (1949) *The English Middle Classes*. London: Phoenix House.

Liversidge, W. (1962) Life chances, *Sociological Review*, 10: 17–34.

Lockwood, D. (1995) Marking out the middle class(es), in T. Butler and M. Savage (eds) *Social Change and the Middle Classes*. London: University College London Press.

Lucey, H. and Reay, D. (2002) Carrying the beacon of excellence, *Journal of Education Policy*, 17(3): 321–36.

Mac an Ghaill, M. (1994) *The Making of Men: Masculinities, Sexualities and Schooling*. Buckingham: Open University Press.

McCaig, C. (2000) New Labour and education, education, education, in M. Smith and S. Ludlum (eds) *New Labour in Government*. Basingstoke: Macmillan.

McCulloch, G. (1998) *Failing the Ordinary Child? The Theory and Practice of Working-class Secondary Education*. Buckingham: Open University Press.

Mack, E. C. (1941) *Public Schools and British Opinion since 1860*. New York: Columbia University Press.

McRobbie, A. (1978) Working class girls and the culture of femininity, in CCCS Women's Studies Group *Women Take Issue*. London: Hutchinson.

Maden, M. (ed.) (2001) *Success Against the Odds Five Years On*. London: Routledge Falmer.

Mahony, P. (1985) *Schools for the Boys? Co-education Reassessed*. London: Hutchinson.

Mann, M. (1993) *The Sources of Social Power Volume II: The Rise of Classes and Nation-states, 1760–1914*. Cambridge: Cambridge University Press.

Marshall, G., Swift, A. and Roberts, S. (1997) *Against the Odds? Social Class and Social Justice in Industrial Societies*. Oxford: Clarendon Press.

Measor, L. and Woods, P. (1984) *Changing Schools*. Milton Keynes: Open University Press.

Mills, C. W. (1961) *The Sociological Imagination*. Harmondsworth: Penguin.

Mills, C. (1995) Managerial and professional work histories, in T. Butler and M. Savage (eds) *Social Change and the Middle Classes*. London: UCL Press.

Morley, L. (1997) Change and equity in higher education, *British Journal of Sociology of Education*, 18(2): 231–42.

Morris, E. (2002) Excellence across sectors. Speech at Institute of Mechanical Engineering, 16 May.

Musgrove, F. (1979) *School and the Social Order*. London: Wiley.

OPCS (1991) *Standard Occupational Classification, Volumes 1, 2 and 3*. London: HMSO.

Papadakis, E. and Taylor-Gooby, P. (1987) *The Private Provision of Public Welfare*. Brighton: Wheatsheaf.

Payne, G. (1987b) *Employment and Opportunity*. London: Macmillan.

Payne, J., with Cheng, Y. and Witherspoon, S. (1998) *Education and Training for 16–18 Year Olds: Individual Paths and National Trends*. London: Policy Studies Institute.

Penlington, G. (2001) Specialist spin that works, *Times Educational Supplement*, 10 August, 9.

Perkin, H. (1989) *The Rise of Professional Society: England since 1880*. London: Routledge.

Power, S. (2000) Educational pathways into the middle class(es), *British Journal of Sociology of Education*, 21(2): 133–45.

Power, S., Edwards, T., Whitty, G. and Wigfall, V. (1998a) Schoolboys and schoolwork: gender identification and academic achievement, *International Journal of Inclusive Education*, 2(2): 135–53.

Power, S., Whitty, G., Edwards, T. and Wigfall, V. (1998b) Schools, families and academically able students: contrasting modes of involvement in secondary education, *British Journal of Sociology of Education*, 19(2): 157–75.

Power, S., Whitty, G., Edwards, T. and Wigfall, V. (1999) Destined for success? Educational biographies of academically able pupils, *Research Papers in Education*, 14(3): 321–39.

Public Schools Commission (1968) *First (Newsom) Report*. London: HMSO.

Public Schools Commission (1970) *Second (Donnison) Report*. London: HMSO.

Rae, J. (1981) *The Public School Revolution: Britain's Independent Schools 1974–79*. London: Faber and Faber.

Redman, P. and Mac an Ghaill, M. (1997) Educating Peter: the making of a history man, in D. L. Steinberg, D. Epstein and R. Johnson (eds) *Border Patrols: Policing the Boundaries of Heterosexuality*. London: Cassell.

Rees, G., Fevre, R., Furlong, J. and Gorard, S. (1997) History, place and the learning society: towards a sociology of lifetime learning, *Journal of Education Policy*, 12(6): 485–97.

Reid, I., Williams, R. and Rayner, M. (1991) The education of the elite, in G. Walford (ed.) *Private Schooling: Tradition, Change and Diversity*. London: Paul Chapman.

Roach, J. (1971) *Public Examinations in England 1850–1900*. Cambridge: Cambridge University Press.

Roberts, K. (1993) Career trajectories and the mirage of increased social mobility, in I. Bates and G. Riseborough (eds) *Youth and Inequality*. Buckingham: Open University Press.

Roberts, K. (2001) *Class in Modern Britain*. Basingstoke: Palgrave.

Roberts, K., Cook, F. G., Clark, S. C. and Semeonoff, E. (1977) *The Fragmentary Class Structure*. London: Heinemann.

Robertson, S. and Lauder, H. (2001) A class choice? Restructuring the education/social class relation, in R. Phillips and J. Furlong (eds) *Education, Reform and the State*. London: Routledge.

Rogers, M. (1994) Grow up lesbian: the role of the school, in D. Epstein (ed.) *Challenging Lesbian and Gay Inequalities in Education*. Buckingham: Open University Press.

Rubinstein, W. (1986) Education and the social origins of British elites 1890–1970, *Past and Present*, 112: 163–207.

Rubinstein, W. (1993) *Capitalism, Culture, and Decline in Britain*. London: Routledge.

Salter, B. and Tapper, T. (1985) *Power and Policy in Education: The Case of Independent Schooling*. Lewes: Falmer Press.

Saran, R. (1973) *Policy Making in Secondary Education: A Case Study*. Oxford: Clarendon Press.

Saunders, P. (1996) *Unequal but Fair? A Study of Class Barriers in Britain*. London: Institute of Economic Affairs, Choice and Welfare Unit.

Saunders, P. (1997) Social mobility in Britain: an empirical evaluation of two competing explanations, *Sociology*, 31(2): 261–88.

Savage, M. (2000) *Class Analysis and Social Transformation*. Buckingham: Open University Press.

Savage, M., Barlow, J., Dickens, P. and Fielding, T. (1992) *Property, Bureaucracy and Culture: Middle Class Formation in Contemporary Britain*. London: Routledge.

Schools Inquiry Commission (1868) *Reports from Commissioner, Volume 13*. London: Eyre & Spottiswoode for Her Majesty's Stationery Office.

Scott, J. (1991) *Who Rules Britain?* Cambridge: Polity Press.

Smithers, A. and Robinson, P. (1997) *Co-educational and Single-sex Schooling – Revisited*. Uxbridge: Brunel University.

Social Exclusion Unit (1999) *Bridging the Gap: New Opportunities for 16–18-year-olds Not in Education, Employment or Training*. London: The Stationery Office.

Spender, D. (1981) Sex bias: in D. Warren Piper (ed.) *Is Higher Education Fair?* Papers presented to the Seventeenth Annual Conference. Guildford: Society for Research into Higher Education.

Sutton Trust (2000) *Entry to Leading Universities*. London: Sutton Trust.

Sutton Trust (2001) *Educational Apartheid: A Practical Way Forward*. London: Sutton Trust.

Swift, D. (1965) Meritocratic and social class selection at age 11, *Educational Research*, 8(1): 65–73.

Tapper, T. (1997) *Fee-paying Schools and Educational Change in Britain*. London: Woburn Press.

Tapper, T. and Salter, B. (1986) The Assisted Places Scheme: a policy evaluation, *Journal of Education Policy*, 1(4): 315–30.

Thomson, G. (1969) *The Education of an Englishman*. Edinburgh: Moray House College of Education.

Tod, I. (1874) *On the Education of Girls of the Middle Classes*. London: William Ridgway.

Turner, R. (1961) Modes of social ascent through education: sponsored and contest mobility, in A. Halsey, J. Floud and A. Anderson (eds) *Education, Economy and Society*. New York: Free Press.

Tyler, W. (1988) *School Organization: A Sociological Perspective*. London: Croom Helm.

Wakeford, J. (1969) *The Cloistered Elite: A Sociological Analysis of the English Public Boarding School*. London: Macmillan.

Walford, G. (1986) *Life in Public Schools*. London: Methuen.

Walford, G. (1989) *Private Schools in Ten Countries*. London: Routledge.

Walford, G. (1991) Private schooling into the 1990s, in G. Walford (ed.) *Private Schooling: Tradition, Change and Diversity*. London: Paul Chapman.

Walford, G. (1993) Girls' private schooling: past and present, in G. Walford (ed.) *The Private Schooling of Girls: Past and Present*. London: Woburn Press.

Walford, G. (ed.) (1994) *Researching the Powerful in Education*. London: UCL Press.

Walford, G. and Jones, S. (1986) The Solihull Adventure: an attempt to reintroduce selective schooling, *Journal of Education Policy*, (3): 239–53.

Walkerdine, V. (1989) Femininity as performance, *Oxford Review of Education*, 15(3): 267–79.

Westergaard, J. and Resler, H. (1975) *Class in a Capitalist Society*. London: Heinemann.

Whitty, G. (1997) *Social Theory and Education Policy: The Legacy of Karl Mannheim*. London: Institute of Education.

Whitty, G., Power, S. and Halpin, D. (1998) *Devolution and Choice in Education: The School, the State and the Market*. Buckingham: Open University Press.

Whitty, G. (2002) *Making Sense of Education Policy*. London: Paul Chapman.

Wiener, M. J. (1981) *English Culture and the Decline of the Industrial Spirit 1850–1980*. Cambridge: Cambridge University Press.

Wilkinson, H. and Mulgan, G. (1995) *Freedom's Children: Work, Relationships and Politics for the 21st Century*. London: Fontana.

Wilkinson, R. (1964) *The Prefects: British Leadership and the Public School Tradition*. Oxford: Oxford University Press.

Willis, P. (1977) *Learning to Labour*. Farnborough: Saxon House.

Willmott, R. (1999) Structure, agency and the sociology of education: rescuing analytical dualism, *British Journal of Sociology of Education*, 20(1): 5–22.

Woods, P. (1977) *The Pupil's Experience, E202, Schooling and Society*. Milton Keynes: Open University Press.

Young, M. (1999) Some reflections on the concepts of social exclusion and inclusion: beyond the Third Way, in A. Hayton (ed.) *Tackling Disaffection and Social Exclusion*. London: Kogan Page.

Index

middle class
  and comprehensive schooling,
    15–18, 31, 39–40, 51, 85
  decampment into private schooling,
    17–18
  divisions within, 2, 7–9, 16–17, 3–2,
    118–19, 125–6, 128–9
  and entry to grammar schools,
    11–13, 15
  growth in 'middle-class'
    employment, 116–17
  neglected in sociology of education,
    1–3, 152
  'old' and 'new', 31–40, 125–6
  professional and managerial
    employment, 118–26, 128
  and public schools, 7–10, 14
Mills, C., 2, 123
Mulgan, G., 145

Newcastle Commission (1861), 7

occupational status of parents, 27, 31,
  161
organic solidarity, individualized and
  personalized, 33–4
Oxford and Cambridge, 83–5, 88–9,
  91–4, 125
  meritocratic entry to, 110–11
  the 'obvious' private school choice,
    109–12
Oxford Mobility Studies, 3, 6, 12,
  15–16

parental choice of school
  and 'old' and 'new' middle classes,
    34–41
  and parental education, 28–32
  parental priorities, 51–3
  and sector of parental employment,
    32–4
participation rates in higher education,
  2, 43–4, 82–3, 117
Payne, G., 117
Payne, J., 43, 45
Perkin, H., 7, 17, 32, 85, 127
political arithmetic, 3

Pollard, S., 15, 17–18, 30, 47, 83, 92,
  127, 151
Power, S., 2, 43, 52, 56, 68–9, 80,
  104, 126
prime career trajectory, 45, 150
private schooling
  academic revolution in, 15, 47, 151
  and choice of degree course, 94–8
  and employment, 122
  protection against downward
    mobility, 45, 102
  and relative advantage, 12, 151–2,
    154
  and sector of employment, 126–8
  social exclusiveness, 14, 57–9
  and university choice, 84, 88–92
  and university entry, 109–15, 124–5
  see also elite private schools; Oxford
    and Cambridge
Public Schools Commission (1968,
  1970), 13–14
public and private sector employment,
  32–3, 126–7
pupils
  academic identies, 53, 55–7, 67–76,
    106–7
  being 'cool' and being 'hard', 71–4
  expectations and perceptions of
    academic success, 102–7
  and friendships, 60, 67–9, 75–6
  involvement in school culture, 22,
    52–3, 57–9, 106
  perceptions of relative failure, 103,
    108–9, 112–15
  and school work, 64–6
  and sport, 70–1, 74
  transition to secondary school, 53–5
  see also gender differences; school
    cultures

rational action, 4–5, 43–4
relative educational advantage, 47–8
Roach, J., 9
Roberts, K., 3, 136
Rubinstein, 8–9, 14, 127

Salter, B., 15, 30
Saran, R., 13

EDUCATION AND SOCIAL CHANGE

Amanda Coffey

• How has education been transformed over recent decades?
• What is the relationship between education and the state in contemporary society?
• What are the consequences of educational change for schools, teachers, parents and learners?

Education and Social Change undertakes a systematic sociological analysis of contemporary educational policy and practice. In doing so it charts the substantial and significant changes that education systems have undergone over recent decades, and places them within a broader context of social change. Thematically structured, the book brings together a diverse body of material from the sociology of education to provide a coherent and logical text. It takes a comprehensive approach, summarizing transformations that have occurred in educational policy, and addressing the consequences for institutions as well as for teachers, parents and learners. The author explores the complex and changing relationships between the state and the processes and practices of education. She also stresses the importance of educational experiences for the (re)production of collective and individual biographies. The result is an invaluable text for sociology and social policy students as well as for education professionals engaged in training or further study.

Contents
Introduction – Auditing education – Parents, consumers and choice – Educational knowledge(s) and the school curriculum – Identities and biographies – Pathways, outcomes and difference – Teachers and teaching – (Re)Defining educational research – References.

160pp   0 335 20068 0 (Paperback)   0 335 20069 9 (Hardback)

EDUCATION IN A POST-WELFARE SOCIETY

Sally Tomlinson

> This book provides a context for understanding educational policies which is currently missing from education and social policy courses. It should be compulsory reading.
>
> Len Barton, University of Sheffield

- What have been the positive and negative effects of education reforms in recent years?
- Why are the moderate successes of state education unrecognised and education portrayed as 'failing' or in crisis?
- How has the reproduction of privilege by education persisted despite a rhetoric of equality and inclusion?

Education in a Post-welfare Society provides a concise and critical overview of education policy, as government in Britain has moved from creating a welfare state to promoting a post-welfare society dominated by private enterprise and competitive markets. Concentrating particularly on the past twenty years, Sally Tomlinson places in context the avalanche of legislation and documentation that has re-formed education into a competitive enterprise in which young people 'learn to compete'. She also demonstrates how a relatively decentralised education system became a system in which funding, teaching and curriculum were centrally controlled, and education narrowed to an economic function. Chronologies of education acts, reports and initiatives are provided at the beginning of the first six chapters. Major legislation is summarised, and an extensive bibliography and annotated suggestions for further reading provide additional guidance. The result is an invaluable resource for students of social policy and education, as well as educational researchers and professionals.

Contents

Introduction – Social democratic consensus? Education 1945–79 – Market forces gather: education 1980–7 – Creating competition: education 1988–94 – The consequences of competition: education 1994–7 – New Labour and education: 1997–2000 – Centralizing lifelong learning – Education and the middle classes – Equity issues: race and gender – Education and the economy – Conclusion: Education in a post-welfare society – References – Index.

224pp   0 335 20288 8 (Paperback)   0 335 20289 6 (Hardback)

RATIONING EDUCATION
POLICY, PRACTICE, REFORM AND EQUITY

David Gillborn and Deborah Youdell

This research should make us extremely sceptical that the constant search for 'higher standards' and for ever-increasing achievement scores can do much more than put in place seemingly neutral devices for restratification.

Michael W. Apple,
John Bascom Professor of Curriculum and Instruction
and Educational Policy Studies, University of Wisconsin, Madison

Recent educational reforms have raised standards of achievement but have also resulted in growing inequalities based on gender, 'race' and social class. School by school 'league tables' play a central role in the reforms. These have created an A-to-C economy where schools and teachers are judged on the proportion of students attaining five or more grades at levels A-to-C. To satisfy these demands schools are embracing new and ever more selective attempts to identify 'ability'. Their assumptions and practices embody a new IQism: a simple, narrow and regressive ideology of intelligence that labels working-class and minority students as likely failures, and justifies rationing provision to support those (often white, middle-class boys) already marked for success.

This book reports detailed research in two secondary schools showing the real costs of reform in terms of the pressures on teachers and the rationing of educational opportunity. It will be important reading for any teacher, researcher or policy maker with an interest inequity in education.

Contents
Education and equity – Reforming education: policy and practice – Ability and economy: defining 'ability' in the A-to-C economy – Selection 11–14: fast groups, 'left over' mixed ability and the subject options process – Selection 14–16: sets, tiers, hidden ceilings and floors – Educational triage and the D-to-C conversion: suitable cases for treatment? – Pupils' experiences and perspectives: living with the rationing of education – Conclusions: rationing education – Notes – References – Name index – Subject index.

272pp   0 335 20360 4 (Paperback)   0 335 20361 2 (Hardback)